European Political, Economic, and Security Issues

Europe and Africa

Similarities and Differences in Security Structures

European Political, Economic, and Security Issues

Additional books in this series can be found on Nova's website under the Series tab.

Additional e-books in this series can be found on Nova's website under the eBooks tab.

African Political, Economic, and Security Issues

Additional books in this series can be found on Nova's website under the Series tab.

Additional e-books in this series can be found on Nova's website under the eBooks tab.

EUROPEAN POLITICAL, ECONOMIC, AND SECURITY ISSUES

EUROPE AND AFRICA

SIMILARITIES AND DIFFERENCES IN SECURITY STRUCTURES

ANIS BAJREKTAREVIC
AND
GIULIANO LUONGO

Copyright © 2017 by Nova Science Publishers, Inc.

All rights reserved. No part of this book may be reproduced, stored in a retrieval system or transmitted in any form or by any means: electronic, electrostatic, magnetic, tape, mechanical photocopying, recording or otherwise without the written permission of the Publisher.

We have partnered with Copyright Clearance Center to make it easy for you to obtain permissions to reuse content from this publication. Simply navigate to this publication's page on Nova's website and locate the "Get Permission" button below the title description. This button is linked directly to the title's permission page on copyright.com. Alternatively, you can visit copyright.com and search by title, ISBN, or ISSN.

For further questions about using the service on copyright.com, please contact:
Copyright Clearance Center
Phone: +1-(978) 750-8400   Fax: +1-(978) 750-4470   E-mail: info@copyright.com

NOTICE TO THE READER

The Publisher has taken reasonable care in the preparation of this book, but makes no expressed or implied warranty of any kind and assumes no responsibility for any errors or omissions. No liability is assumed for incidental or consequential damages in connection with or arising out of information contained in this book. The Publisher shall not be liable for any special, consequential, or exemplary damages resulting, in whole or in part, from the readers' use of, or reliance upon, this material. Any parts of this book based on government reports are so indicated and copyright is claimed for those parts to the extent applicable to compilations of such works.

Independent verification should be sought for any data, advice or recommendations contained in this book. In addition, no responsibility is assumed by the publisher for any injury and/or damage to persons or property arising from any methods, products, instructions, ideas or otherwise contained in this publication.

This publication is designed to provide accurate and authoritative information with regard to the subject matter covered herein. It is sold with the clear understanding that the Publisher is not engaged in rendering legal or any other professional services. If legal or any other expert assistance is required, the services of a competent person should be sought. FROM A DECLARATION OF PARTICIPANTS JOINTLY ADOPTED BY A COMMITTEE OF THE AMERICAN BAR ASSOCIATION AND A COMMITTEE OF PUBLISHERS.

Additional color graphics may be available in the e-book version of this book.

Library of Congress Cataloging-in-Publication Data

ISBN: 978-1-53612-337-1

Published by Nova Science Publishers, Inc. † New York

"*Europe needs new models of articulation. From vertical hierarchies, the European world of preponderance today must rethink the new horizontal organization in the sociology of international relations. The authors of this book bravely, clearly, and repeatedly point this out.*"

Slavko Kulić, Prof. Dr. SC., IOM, St. Catherine Oxford, Institute on World Problems for Europe

"*This well researched and well-structured book provides a clear and up to date perspective on 'forgotten continent', issue so much missing from the contemporary literature. By skillfully contrasting and com-paring the 'forgotten' with an 'old' continent, the authors have accomplished a real feat. Anyone who is interested in African and/or security studies will find this book as an indispensable reader. For scholars dealing with the geopolitics of Africa and Eurasia this will be a must read for many years to come.*"

Prof. Alexander Zistakis, PhD, University of Athens, Greece

CONTENTS

Foreword A ix
          Tomislav Jakić

Foreword B xiii
          Emanuel L. Paparella

Preface xix

List of Abbreviations xxi

Chapter 1	Introduction	1
Chapter 2	European Imperialism	3
Chapter 3	Institutionalization of Historical Experiences in Africa	27
Chapter 4	Institutionalization of Historical Experiences in Europe	69
Chapter 5	Similarities and Differences in Africa and Europe	93
Chapter 6	Conclusion and Analysis of Hypothesis	99

Future Outlook 109

Afterword 111

References 113

Author Profiles 127

Index 129

FOREWORD A

"A MUCH NEEDED BOOK"

Tomislav Jakić
Former Foreign Policy Advisor to the
Croatian President Stjepan Mesić

"Our history warns. Nevertheless, it also provides a hope." In this one short sentence is the essence of the book "Europe and Africa" written by Anis Bajrektarevic and Giuliano Luongo. The book combines in a unique way both the past and the present of two continents, which are quite different – in almost every aspect – now, but which were deeply interconnected during the colonial past – with Europe influencing Africa and Africa planting the seeds of influence on Europe that will be unveiled many years after.

The book concentrates on security structures on both continents, trying to answer the question why Europe is multilateral and Africa still bilateral in this field. The authors examine the historical experiences and look in them for causes of today's developments. Special emphasis is put on both World Wars, in which Europe and Africa took part, but in a quite different way, having in mind that the majority of African states became independent only after WW 2. While in Africa foreign powers for centuries dictated what, where and how is going to happen, Europe was never in a situation in which foreign elements would or could determine its development.

Failures of both colonial and post-colonial period are the main causes, so the authors argue, for conflicts and security problems in today's Africa. However, on both continents economic and political stability are the condition sine qua non for peace and security.

The authors clearly distinguish between the way Europe was (and is) developing and the way Africa does (still very much following a model abandoned n Europe years ago). They point out how the Cold war influenced things in Europe, but not in Africa, thus resulting in a different approach to security questions. They analyze the regional organizations and their character.

Special emphasis is put on integration processes in Europe and Africa and the reasons why Africa is far away from the European Union (despite the current state of the EU and several attempts to put into life something similar to the EU in Africa). Asian security structures and the reasons why they are as they are, did not escape the focus of the authors, although they are primarily dealing with Europe and Africa, always searching – with good reason - for the roots of today's situation in the European past, going back even to the times of Roman empire.

The central message of the book is formulated in the following quotation: "For a serious advancement of multilateralism, mutual trust, a will to compromise and achieve a common denominator through active co-existence is the key. It is hard to build a common course of action around the disproportionately big and centrally positioned member which would escape the interpretation as containment by the big or assertiveness of its center by the smaller, peripheral members."

But, better than anything else the authors formulate their "philosophy" in the already mentioned sentence: "Our history warns. Nevertheless, it also provides a hope."

Hope is based on knowledge. In addition, whoever wants to know, should read the book "Europe and Africa". It explains not only what happened in the past, but also what and why is happening today.

And this is why this book is "much needed".

FOREWORD B

Emanuel L. Paparella
Professor
Barry University, Miami, FL, US

This book is the kind of geo-political treatise that will take the reader down the byways of a millennial interface between two proximate and inextricably intertwined continents.

Geologists surmise that the earth is approximately 7 billion years old. Its five continents were once one. Then they began to break up. Europe divided from Africa with the Mediterranean Sea in between them as a water boundary of sorts. Italy, for example, which is now part of Europe was an island derived from Africa floating in the Mediterranean Sea, which then collided with the European continent forming the Alps that separate that peninsula from the rest of the European continent. Not many people realize that there are parts of Southern Sicily which are on a lower latitude than parts of Tunisia, the home of ancient Carthage, in Africa. That's how proximate Africa is to Europe.

My father was an agronomist by profession who after World War II worked for the Italian government for a good 15 years of his life. Part of his professional duties was that of helping with the supervising of the agrarian reform the government conducted in the 50s on behalf of farmers who were assigned parcels of unused land expropriated from rich landowners. Sometimes he would take me along in his car. I was ten or twelve at the time. As he supervised the agricultural planning he would grab a fistful of earth and would show it to me exclaiming: "you see this land, it is land from Africa; the whole of Italy is covered with land from Africa." Before World War II he had hoped to go use his expertise in an Italian colony of the times: Eritrea on the horn of Africa, but that never came to pass.

By the way, this process of land from Africa literally landing in Europe is still an ongoing process. The Scirocco is a wind blowing into Italy out of Africa that carries with it sand and earth on a regular basis. Indeed, historically speaking, Italy from the outset has functioned as a bridge between the two continents on both a geo-political and an historical level. To be convinced of this all one needs to do is travel to the island of Lampedusa situated between Sicily and Africa and you'll witness with your own eyes the greatest migration of people between two continents ongoing on a daily basis as we speak.

The human exodus allegedly began out of Africa some ten thousand years ago, so in that respect that makes us all Africans. Tell that to KKK members! But then again there are some doubts, given that skeletons of a primitive man living 800,000 years ago have been found in Northern Greece. Be that as it may, on a purely civilizational level, cultures residing in Africa (which includes Egypt) and Europe have always confronted and often clashed with each other. One thinks of the Second Punic War in 200 BC with Carthage situated in present day Tunisia, with Hannibal challenging the might of the Roman Empire; a challenge picked up by Publius Cornelius Scipio, the African so called, who eventually defeated Hannibal and destroyed Carthage. Egypt is later absorbed into the empire as is also Greece. So we end with Greco-

Roman culture which later synthesizes with a religion from the Middle East, Christianity, giving rise to a unique European medieval civilization which metamorphoses into the Renaissance, a synthesis of antiquity and Christianity, followed by the Enlightenment and the rise of modern liberalism.

But to go back to Africa. At the height of Western European imperialism in the 17th, 18th and 19th century, Africa becomes a playfield for Western colonial powers: France, the Netherland, England, Germany, Spain, Italy and Belgium. These powers were fiercely nationalistic with their own languages and cultures. Africa might have been racially heterogeneous but lacked nationalism; that was a unique "gift" bestowed on it by the colonial powers. The question arises: how did it effect the subsequent African nationalism? Was it a question of passing from colony to nationhood? The fact is that some of those present day nations of Africa have never been colonies; some had an ancient culture prior to their brief stint as colonies. This is a conundrum of sorts but we need to go beyond it.

The political arrangement of Africa prior to the advent of the Europeans was the tribal system. Now, there are some tribes, such as the Hutu and the Tutsi, whose origins and long-term location span what today are 17 nations. One is hard put to find a time in recorded history when those tribes were gathered together as a single geo-political entity, a mega-nation of sorts or even a confederacy. It's a situation similar to that of Native Americans. There were at time alliances of tribes but never a veritable confederacy. Undoubtedly, there was little nationalism in Africa prior to European colonization. The norm was persistent periodic tribal wars; even in tools, artifacts and artistic expression, there was little permanent long-term national identity, so called.

Part of the "gift" of progress which Europeans boast of having bestowed on Africa were infrastructural nationalistic elements such as a common language, education, governance, transportation, reliable food and water. To be sure, those things did not exist in the tribal era. Which is to say, for the European it was a sign that "progress" and its inevitability had arrived in Africa and as per Enlightenment, progress is unstoppable, and deterministic. But was it real progress? Is anything that is determined and limits man's freedom ever desirable, always positive and progressive? That is of course a philosophical question based, in this case, on geo-political considerations. Let's see.

With the end of colonialism you have the birth of a plethora of new African nations (see map below) and new nationals who, alas, were ill prepared for nationalism but were elevated to positions of leadership. The national differences with neighboring countries remain in fact the old tribal differences as exacerbated by European colonialism. The new unprepared leaders simply imitated the former masters and colonizers. The clever by half tactic was simply that of the old masters, divide and conquer: rallying one group against another. Nationalism is a mere by-product. It would be hard to find people willing to argue that any of the sub-Saharan nations on today's map are models of utopian societies to which neighbors wish to emigrate or wishing to form national federations a la EU.

Understanding the adoption of "divide and rule" and the sense of hatred induced among the tribes by the colonists helps us understand better the conflict in Rwanda, for example. Both Hutu and Tutsi live in Rwanda. Germany and Belgium took control and divided people who in reality had the same fundamental culture, religion and language. The distinguishing marks now became their height, shape of nose and other racial banalities. Some Africans are now declared super-races meant to keep the inferior races down. The ultimate result was genocide from which the Europeans, who had produced a monstrous one of their own only a few decades before, rather hypocritically professed to be scandalized, but for whose avoidance they did not lift a finger. It was nationalism, not tribalism which caused the disaster.

That kind of division continues today, unfortunately. The division is now among political parties who disseminate propaganda of hatred of one group against another. Those are stories one will not find in publishing houses but at the fire-place passed on from one generation to the other. They are the bitter fruits of colonialism with their roots in nationalism which often established artificial borderlines ignoring the cultures of local communities. The new leaders meanwhile may not be foreigners but are much like the old crooked manipulative colonialists.

To land communally held, new structures were put in place with far reaching economic implications for the natives. Land laws remain in dire need of reform. If nationalism is understood as local pride and heroism, and a quest for autonomy, then patriotism is not lacking in Africa if one is to judge from various rebellions: the Lamogi rebellion in Uganda, the Ndebele rebellion in Zimbabwe, the vita ya maji rebellion in Tanzania, not to speak of those professionals patriots whose expertise could be making them a bundle of money in the USA or Europe, but choose to stay in their native African countries to help their communities.

Within this analysis and context, which are neither Utopian nor Machiavellian, but realistic, we may now ask: how can the above mentioned book function as a guide to improved relations between Europe and Africa? Are those relations improvable by comparing the geo-political situation of both continents? This book seems to answer with an optimistic yes. Perhaps that is the right answer but only if the Europeans first acknowledge the original failures of European imperialism and colonialism and its exploitative practices. Which is to say, no solution is feasible to the present acute problems of refugees and terrorism, just to mention two, unless the ones who produced the problem in the first place with their doctrines of power and domination, acknowledge that they have been guilty in the past of the initial African geo-political problem. Without that acknowledgment they run the risk of remaining perennially part of the problem rather than part of the solution.

This book could indeed function as an initial step to forge security structures built on horizontal rather than vertical hierarchical underpinnings with emphasis on international cooperation rather than rivalry, to prepare a smoother more coherent transition from tribal to national system without falling into rabid nationalism, perhaps acknowledging that not every transition from tribal to national is necessarily desirable. That's how it could be interpreted, and perhaps it is the only way it can be interpreted and thus result beneficial to future European-African interactions.

We know full well what rabid nationalism and ideology wrought to Europe only 70 years ago. It is imperative that its consequences be not repeated in Africa and this for the sake of both continents. In some way, the scope of this book is Cassandrian, to warn Europeans to remember their own history and not to repeat their mistakes in Africa. But let us also keep in mind that Cassandra, while gifted by the gods with the gift of prophecy, the ability to predict the future and warn people about impending doom, was at the same time afflicted by the gods with a curse: few people took her warnings seriously. It was an unrecognized gift.

Be that as it may, this is the kind of book that needs to be read and pondered, discussed and debated carefully and seriously. If that is done, it may well clarify quite a few unsolved geo-political puzzles of the bizarre and confusing times in which we live and have our being.

PREFACE

Europe, with its highly integrated international networks, belongs nowadays to the most secure areas of the world in the matter of localized regional conflicts. On the opposite end, there is the poorest continent – namely, Africa – with the least developed international structure and with the highest number of armed conflicts in the world.

The aim of this book is to examine the historic development of security structures on these two diverse continents, as well as their similarities and differences. The first part of the text focuses on the historic development of Europe and Africa and their interrelations. The second part describes the European and African security structures. The last part covers the similarities and differences between the two security systems.

The text shows the economic and political interdependence of European states that was mainly established through the foundation of several supranational institutions after the Second World War in order to ensure sustainable peace and economic prosperity. By contrast, Africa still has serious security problems, and the development of international acting institutions that may help to support stability and peace is still in its infancy.

The contemporary development in Europe will bring the continent even closer together and further boost consolidation among European nations. Due to the absence of a functioning multilateral structure and a basic network of collective security in Africa, states there will have to rely on regional arrangements to balance existing power differences. Nevertheless, in order to obtain economic growth and promote general welfare, a network of multilateral operating institutions is unavoidable.

LIST OF ABBREVIATIONS

AFRC	Armed Forces Revolutionary Council
AIDS	Acquired Immunodeficiency Syndrome
ALDE	Alliance of Liberals and Democrats for Europe
AMISOM	African Union Mission in Somalia
ASSN	African Security Sector Network
AU	African Union
CDD	Center for Development and Democracy
CDS	Defence and Security Commission
CEWARN	Early Warning and Early Response Mechanism
CoE	Council of Europe
COPAX	Council for Peace and Security in Central Africa
CPCC	Civilian Planning and Conduct Capabilities
EASBRIG	Eastern African Standby Brigade
ECCAS	Economic Community of Central African States
ECOMOG	Economic Community of West African States Monitoring Group
ECOWAS	Economic Community of West African States
EDG	European Democrat Group
EEC	European Economic Community
EITI	Extractive Industries Transparency Initiative

EPC	European Political Cooperation
EPP	European People's Party
ESDP	European Security and Defence Policy
EU	European Union
EUMC	European Union Military Committee
EUMS	European Union Military Staff
FLS	Front Line States
FOMAC	Central African multinational force
GATT	General Agreement on Tariffs and Trade
HIV	Human Immunodeficiency Virus
HoSG	Heads of State and Government
IBRD	International Bank for Reconstruction and Development
ICPAT	IGAD Capacity Building Programme Against Terrorism
IGAD	Inter-Governmental Authority on Development
IMF	International Monetary Fund
ISDSC	Inter-State Defence and Security Co-operation
ISPDC	Interstate, Politics and Diplomacy Committee
ISS	Institute for Security Studies
ITO	International Trade Organization
MARAC	Central African multinational force
MCO	Ministerial Committee of the Organ
MCPMR	Mechanism for Conflict Prevention, Management and Resolution
MDGs	Millennium Development Goals
NATO	North Atlantic Treaty Organization
NEPAD	New Partnership for Africa´s Development
NGO	Non Governmental Organization
NSDAP	Nationalsozialistische Deutsche Arbeiterpartei
OAU	Organization of African Unity
OIC	Organization for Islamic Conference

List of Abbreviations

OPDSC	SADC Organ on Politics, Defence and Security Cooperation
OSCE	Organization for Security and Cooperation in Europe
PRC	Permanent Representatives Committee
PSC	Political and Security Committee
REC	Regional Economic Community
REFORM	Regional Food Security and Risk Management Program
RUF	Revolutionary United Front
SADC	Southern African Development Community
SADD	Southern African Development Co-ordination Conference
SASS	South African Secret Service
SEC	Single European Act
SOC	Socialist Group
SRO	Sub-Regional Office
UEL	Group of the Unified European Left
UN	United Nations
UNAMSIL	United Nations Mission to Sierra Leone
UNDP	United Nations Development Program
UNECA	United Nations Economic Commission for Africa
UNIOSIL	United Nations Integrated Office for Sierra Leone
UNO	United Nations Organization
US	Untied States
USA	United States of America
USSR	Union of Sovereign Soviet Republics
WB	World Bank
WEU	Western European Union
WFP	World Food Program
WTO	World Trade Organization
WWI	World War One
WWII	World War Two

Chapter 1

INTRODUCTION

This book will investigate how and why security structures – and their successful implementation – in Europe and Africa are varying to such a wide extent.

Specifically, this work aims at answering the two underlying research questions:

1. Why multilateralism in Europe has developed to such a large extent?
2. Why Africa is bilateral in its security constellations?

With regard to the research question the following hypotheses have been developed:

1.1) Common historical experiences are a precondition for the creation of a comprehensive security framework;
1.2) A stable economic and political environment is the key determinant for the success of regional security structures;
2.1) Symmetry of countries' area and balance of power does not ensure development of multilateral structures;

2.2) Multilateralism is not successfully achieved due to a low degree of trust among African countries;
2.3) The cooperation among African countries is insufficient due to contradictory interests and needs of different African countries.

Given the two continents' geographical proximity and Europe's strong influence on Africa over the centuries, it might have been supposed that both continents would have experienced similar developments. However, regarding peace and security Europe claims today one of the most multilateralized security structures internationally while Africa is still struggling to establish an effective security framework.

The first part of the text focuses on the historic development of Europe and Africa and their interrelations beginning in the 17th century, which was dominated by European colonialism. An analysis of the European competition for the African continent and its resulting implications provides a base for understanding the present situation of Africa. Africa is analysed with a focus on former Portuguese, French, British, Belgian, German and Italian colonies. Analysis starts with Africa's institutionalization of historical experiences based on the development of bilateral and multilateral security structures, as well as looking at the regional security organizations, the concepts of collective security and collective defence, up to the contemporary international order. In a similar way, the institutionalization of historical experiences in Europe is discussed.

The fourth part primarily deals with the similarities and differences of those two security structures. Finally, the conclusion sums up the most important findings of this book and provides arguments to answer the research questions and approve or refute the hypotheses.

Chapter 2

EUROPEAN IMPERIALISM

2.1. EUROPEAN COLONIZATION OF AFRICA

The colonization of the African continent by European powers occurred in several waves. In the 15th century, the Spanish and the Portuguese empires started to cautiously explore and colonize the African continent. Also, first trade activities were established primarily through African middlemen, who traded spices and fruits grown on the African continent, and slaves. Additionally, Europeans seized contacts, which were able to supply them with gold, especially from the area of present-day Ghana.

The second wave of colonization took place in the 17th century, during the time the British and the French empires were showing increased interest in Africa. At the end of the 17th century, the European powers were already heavily dependent on trade with the Africans- especially on trade in slaves, and gold, which was needed to support trading activities with the Asian continent. In addition, the trade in commodities, e.g., palm oil, cloves, and in luxury goods like ivory, became more important over time.

In the middle of the 19th century, even the Belgian king began to acquire territory on the African continent, in order to stay competitive with other European powers, mostly with the French empire. The "late coming" European colonizers (German and Italian empires) arrived in Africa in the mid to late 19th century.

Nevertheless, the European empires were unable to expand their rule effectively over the African continent before the 19th century, especially due to two main factors.

In the first place, permanent settling in Africa was not taken as a priority, due to weather and climate-related conditions, and to the presence of various diseases, which could not be efficiently countered at the time. In the second place, the African indigenous tribes did not want to comply with the European colonizers and successfully opposed them on various occasions (MacKenzie, 1983).

2.2. EUROPE IN THE 19TH CENTURY

The delay in the African "conquest" by Europe was also due to another very relevant factor: the notable social and political instability on the European continent, which translated in the civil wars and revolutions of the 18th and 19th century – among these, the most notorious example is the French revolution of the 1790s, capable of overthrowing the monarchy and establishing a constitutional government. Furthermore, in the early 19th century many national movements rose, promoting revolutionary activity.

Also, many external conflicts were experienced, too. The Belgian revolution of 1830 highlighted the growing national movement and the desire for independence of the Belgium population from the United Kingdom of the Netherlands. In addition, European rivalries (e.g., Anglo-French) played a role in Europe in 19th century. (Pilbeam, 1995)

2.3. REASONS FOR EUROPEAN COLONIZATION

At first, the European powers exercised their trading activities and informal control primarily on the African coasts. They did not feel a need to expand their positions further inside, since African intermediaries provided goods from the inland. In the second half of the 19th century, the European colonizers noticed that political instability (especially on riverside areas) had a huge influence on European-African trading activities. Europeans started to believe that trade from the African interior should be mainly controlled by them, in order to minimize their dependency from intermediaries. To obtain a better knowledge of the continent, they initiated many explorations to the unknown areas of Africa. During explorations, they realized the market potential of the African interior as a supplier of raw materials and labor: this awareness together with the economic depression of the 1870s triggered the competition of European powers for the African continent.

European powers viewed the markets of the African continent as rich of resources with high potential and various investment possibilities. The increase of applied capital in the African economy was accompanied by the desire of European powers to have a high economic and political control over these markets.

Also, non-economic motivations played an important role. In the second half of the 19th century the slave trade was abolished, but African indigenous people still were a part of European armies: thus, protracted expansion was seen as a feasible method for conscription in national armies. Another non-economic factor was the empowerment of national prestige: a country's reputation was improved by acquiring new territories abroad. (Sanderson, 1985, p.96-p.117)

Khapoya (1998) also mentions the relevance of the "prestige" factor, next to the need for spreading religion – and, with it, its related "pressure power" – as well as the need for increased knowledge about the African territory and its potential for exploitation.

2.4. PARTITION OF THE AFRICAN CONTINENT

In the late 19th century discovered market potential of African center increased competition on an already hostile continent. Other than "partition", this competition for the control of Africa is also informally called "scramble for Africa": under the temporal point of view, this period is identified as running from 1884 to 1914. By the end of 1914, around 90% of the African continent went under European control, while in 1870 has been estimated that Europeans controlled roughly the 10% of the continent. Shillington (2005) additionally notes that this is the period when the transition from "informal imperialism" to the direct rule of "colonial imperialism" took place.

The very beginning of this European competition was dominated by the French and British empires, which competed for various territories in the West and central Africa. Meanwhile, King Leopold II of Belgium urged to bring a relevant part of central Africa (the area of Congo) under his control[1]. This ignited a huge conflict among the European powers, especially the British and French, which also competed for this territory[2]. This dispute concerning the central African territory led Otto von Bismarck (the first chancellor of Germany) to call for an international conference in Berlin aiming to assure colonial borders and

---

[1] In 1876, King Leopold II invited British explorer Henry Morton Stanley to join him to explore the continent on his behalf. The King founded two years later the International Association of the Congo (in French: Association Internationale du Congo, also known as International Congo Society) as a replacement for the Committee for the Study of the Upper Congo (French: Comité d'études du Haut-Congo). The new association shifted goals more towards the economic profit instead of geographic research.

[2] On behalf of France, the Italian explorer Pietro Savorgnan di Brazzà (who later took French nationality) signed an agreement with King Iloo of the Teke (the Brazzà-Makoko Treaty) in the upper Congo area, giving the chance to French government of extending their influence on the area. In order to stop French expansionism, the British Empire supported Portuguese territorial revendications: on February 1883, Great Britain and Portugal signed a treaty in which the first recognized the sovereignty of the latter on the entire mouth of the river Congo.

ease current and potential future disputes. This Berlin Conference was held in 1884, and next to Germany saw the participation of Great Britain, France, Portugal, Netherlands, Belgium, Spain and the United States. With a minor role, among participants were also Italy, the United Kingdoms of Sweden and Norway, Russia, and the Ottoman Empire.

There, the main European powers agreed on a division of the African continent among them thereby ignoring all traditional and indigenous structures and borders. "Spheres of influence" enabled the Europeans to exercise their political and economic rule, by putting European norms in place, which the indigenous Africans had to obey. This repression broke African self-esteems and terminated African resistance. (Djamson, 1976, p.249-255)

This act, for the first time in history, took African politics and matters on a global level. One chapter of this agreement required the European powers to care about the well-being and the improvement of the living conditions of indigenous tribes under its respective flag. Another chapter covered the complex issue of trade regulation: European powers agreed to permit free trade on the African continent, and to make all coastlines accessible to all European empires. Moreover, the Europeans agreed on the creation of a Congo Free State, which was under political and economic rule of Leopold II of Belgium. The Belgian king had to assure free trade in this area for all other European powers. (Sanderson, 1985, p.135-p.138)

The upcoming pages are explaining French, Belgian, German, Italian, British and Portuguese positions in more detail.

2.4.1. Portuguese Empire

Portugal was first empire that explored Africa (15th century). Portugal was a small country if compared with the other powers at the time, and its resources were relatively limited. Portugal managed to keep control on the areas it first explored because no other power wanted to seize them or, as mentioned earlier, because the British Empire found it convenient to support Portuguese control. Portuguese colonialism was characterized by forced labour. Administration was centralized by press censorship, police repression and the suppression of all forms of democracy. Portuguese colonialism can be split in three macro-periods or eras, classified as the following: first era (1415-1663), covering the early incursions in Africa and south-eastern Asia, next to expeditions towards the Americas; second era (1663-1825), characterized by further incursions in South America (mainly Brazil); third era (1822-1999), mostly defined by the decline and ultimate fall of the country's colonial empire.

In Africa, Portugal managed to acquire the territories of present-day Cape Verde, Guinea, Sao Tome and Principe, Angola and Mozambique.

It has been reported that Portugal nursed the dream of ruling Africa "forever": aside from the propaganda of the time, it is interesting to point out that the Portuguese Empire lasted from 1415 to 1974-75 – additionally, some historians prefer to indicate the ultimate collapse date on 2002, with the grant of sovereignty to East Timor.

The ten islands of Cape Verde were colonized by Portugal in the 15th century and used especially as a trading centre for African slaves, which were also used to grow cotton and indigo in the previously uninhabited Cape Verde islands. (cf. CIA Factbook, 2009, n.p.a). The country became independent in 1975 due to the collapse of the Portuguese empire after the Carnation Revolution in Lisbon in 1974 (Foreign & Commonwealth Office, 2009, n.p.a).

2.4.2. French Empire

French colonizers arrived on the African continent in the 17th century, exercising trading activities in West Africa[3] in their first decades of presence. A stronger colonial effort came from France only in the 19th century, when – after the fall enfeeblement of the Ottoman Empire – it managed to enter in Algeria and take control of its capital, Algiers, in 1830.

Only in the early 19th century, the French were beginning to conquer and colonize Africa. After the Berlin Conference, several territories came under the control of France: at the height of its colonial power, it controlled various

French-controlled territories spanned all over the African continent. The main administrative divisions, mostly denominated after the geographical position, were the following:

- French North Africa, controlling the territories of Maghreb (present-day Morocco, Algeria and Tunisia);
- French West Africa ("*Afrique Occidentale Française, AOF*"), formed by the territories of Ivory Coast (*Cote d'Ivoire*), Dahomey (named Benin after obtaining independence in 1960), French Sudan[4], Guinea, Mauritania, Senegal, Upper Volta (named Burkina Faso from 1984), Niger, French Togoland[5], James Island and Albreda[6];
- French Equatorial Africa ("*Afrique Équatoriale Française, AEF*"), under whose administration fell the territories of Chad, Gabon, French Congo[7], Ubangi-Shari[8], and French Cameroon[9];

---

[3] Mainly in the area of present-day Senegal.
[4] The colony of French Sudan corresponds to present-day Mali. It took its current name in 1960.
[5] Controlled by France under the mandate of the League of Nations, 1916-1960.
[6] Islands in the Gambia River. James Island has been renamed Kunta Kinteh Island in 2011, thanks to the effort of the artist Chaz Guest.
[7] Also known as "Middle Congo" or "Congo Brazzaville" in some references.

- French Comoros, comprising the islands of Anjouan, Grande Comore, and Mohéli. Lying near the northern end of the Mozambique Channel, these islands form the present-day nation of Comoros;
- additionally, France controlled the French Somaliland[10], Madagascar, and – for a relatively short time – the island of Mauritius[11].
- Differently from other territories, AOF and AEF were proper federation of colonies, being ruled by a single governor, who directly reported to the central government in Paris[12].

AOF administration system was the "general model" of colonial administration for French territories. It was based on the system of "circles"[13]. A variable number of smaller administrative divisions called "cantons" composed each circle; a single canton was composed by various villages.

Circles were led by a Commander ("*Commandant de cercle*"), not dependant from the military structure but subject to the authority of the colony's government about civil affairs. Circle Commanders had the power to appoint (and remove) local chiefs (for example, village chiefs) nominated among African locals. These chiefs were mostly appointed on the basis of their – supposed or not – loyalty to France, not on existing rights on role in the local society.

---

[8] This colony took his name because it was established in the area of the rivers Ubangi and Chari. Its territories were renamed Central African Republic (CAR) in 1958, and took independence on the 13th of August, 1960.

[9] French Cameroon was another League of Nations mandate. It is currently part of present-day Cameroon.

[10] Known as French Territory of the Afars and the Issas in 1967 and renamed Djibouti after its independence in 1977.

[11] Mauritius was named "*Ile de France*" (lit. "Island of France") during the French colonial rule between 1715 and 1814.

[12] The Ministry of Colonies was the main liaison administration entity on the matter.

[13] "*Cercles*" in French.

From 1934, differently from AOF, AEF was transformed in a unified colony with a single, colony-wide budget; its administrative divisions were called "regions" and then "territories".

The French colonial doctrine is defined by the so-called "assimilation" policy. The theory of assimilation stated that colonial domination would have transformed institutions and customs of the indigenous peoples, pushing them towards the habits of the *"civilization française"*. In this way, the assimilation doctrine was coherent with the Jacobin conception of the Republic in France[14].

The assimilation policy founded itself on the inequality of races, the domination and the exploitation of colonies: these acts were perceived as legitimate in the name of the "natural law". France assumed the right and "duty" of imposing the colonial rule as a mean to abolish war and slavery via the policies of *"mise en valeur"*[15]. The French colonial power took the tutelage of the African people[16] to make them "French citizens" (or *citoyens*). The colonial system was generally centralized and hierarchic; it applied the rule of *"indigénat"* (translatable in "the condition of being indigenous"), a condition establishing that colonial authorities could impose criminal sanctions to the indigenous people without recurring to tribunals.

Additionally, the assimilation did not recognize indigenous chief of state. Only after World War I, French colonizers gave recognition to locals called *"chefs coutumiers"*. The fragmentation of centralized political systems brought to the birth of completely artificial territorial and administrative divisions. The territorial unity was considered as a fundamental integration factor for the civilization process. In the regions controlled by Muslim elites, collaboration with indigenous

---

[14] The Jacobins, also known as the Society of Jacobins or – until 1792 – the Society of the Friends of the Constitution, were a very influential political club active in France in the revolutionary era.
[15] By *"mise en valeur"* (literally: "valorisation"), French colonizers meant a series of policy acts finalized to improve the structural/infrastructural conditions of an area.
[16] Interestingly, French colonizers used the term *sujets* (literally "subjects") to address African indigenous people, subtly having a pejorative meaning.

chiefs was very important for the establishment of colonial institutions.[17]

Early reforms of the colonial administration led to some forms of reconnaissance of the authority of indigenous peoples at lower levels. The colonizers chose for administrative positions locals who, under the French point of views, understood the "*choses des blancs*" (lit. "things of the whites"): soldiers, traders, interpreters, whom the colonizers felt ready and better prepared in working with colonial public affairs. The first infrastructures were created (roads, postal networks, schools…), but they were located only in specific regions which colonizers wanted to support. The population was forced to pay taxes and undertake forced jobs – job rules excluded forced labour, but serfdom and slavery could still be put into practice. Regarding taxation, one of the most notable examples is the one of the "head tax", due to the colonial rulers by every inhabitant above ten years. Similar policies began especially in the less "profitable" areas of West Africa, where the lack of exploitable resources for trade pushed the colonial authorities into taking such decisions (Devereux, 2005). Furthermore, any administration could enforce special tasks.

In 1848, the French government adapted the structure of the administration of the Maghreb territory in order to improve its control. It divided the territory into three provinces, with each province being subdivided into a military and a civil territory. The military territories of the three provinces were governed by three respective generals, who had to assure a proper defensive system and deal with Arabs moving through French territory. The civil parts were administered by prefects, who were responsible for dealing with the settled natives. The supreme

---

[17] Interestingly, coerced cohabitation between Muslim and non-Muslim populations pushed the first into moving in communities headed by chiefs with "mystical" features. This phenomenon led to the birth of religious brotherhoods, sometimes against, sometimes favourable to the colonial administration. Even if the majority of Muslim leaders cooperated with colonizers, various revolts against foreigners exploded: often, they were suppressed by colonial authorities and their chiefs executed.

authority of both, generals and prefects, was the governor-general who was executing the orders of the French empire. The Maghreb territory was the first one in which the French empire established its colonial rule. (Morell, 1854, p.382-383)

The West African region was the largest area to come under colonial rule. In the second half of the 19th century, the French government was trying to expand its position from the West African coast into the centre, by establishing treaties with several chiefs of indigenous tribes. Once a new territory fell under French rule, it was initially administered by army officials. However, in 1891 the extent of expansion required for a more complex administration. Therefore, like already done in the Maghreb territory, the French government put a governor-general into place, which was responsible for executing commands from the French empire. In 1904, the French established a base for the governor-general in Dakar, Senegal so the governor-general got a full power to deal with all issues related to the West African colony. This was a major step towards the idea of independent, self-controlling colonies. With this change, the remaining small powers that were given to the chiefs of indigenous tribes were withdrawn.

After the Berlin Conference, French empire was allocated an area of land ranging from the Congo Free State to the central Sahara. This land was very poor and missed infrastructure: consequently, most French economic actors seemed not interested in this territory. Therefore, the French government created the *"Comité de l'Afrique Française"* (lit.: Committee for French Africa) in 1890, in order to increase the interest and to assist further missions in this territory. In this colony, the French applied the same federal system which was already installed in French West Africa. French Equatorial Africa was divided into four parts, which were governed by the governor-general from a central base in Brazzaville. In this colony French faced the same problems as in others: lack of human and fiscal resources, low profit margins in poor territory. Therefore the French government allowed companies to establish commercial monopolies in French Equatorial Africa. As a return the government received a fee and 15% of the generated profit. This money was used to pay for bodies, e.g., colonial administration and the French police in this territory. (Devereux, 2005, p.260)

2.4.3. British Empire

The British colonial experience in Africa began in the late XVII century, with the establishment of the Royal African Company[18]. British activities, principally located in West Africa, mainly involved slave trade next to the trade of commodities.

The British Empire, at the height of its expansion, spanned through the whole African continent: its territories were located in West, East, North and South Africa. Often, many territories were contended between other colonial powers, with a particularly strong rivalry with France.

At the Berlin Conference in 1884, the area of present-day Kenya was passed under British colonial control. The British government established a Protectorate for East Africa and made Kenya in 1920 a colony of the British Crown. The British took extensive tracks of the best land from Africans, reserved them for white settlers, and denied the dispossessed Africans political participation. Protests by Africans against white settler domination and British rule peaked in 1952 and 1956 and led to an increased African representation in the colony's legislative council. (cf. Library of Congress, 2007, p.2).

In 1806, the British took the Cape (South Africa) in order to protect the sea route to their Asian empire. They tried to keep the costs low and the settlement small. Local officials continued the policy of relying on imported slave labour rather than encouraging European immigration.

---

[18] The Royal African Company was a mercantile company established in 1660 by the Stuart family in London and led by James, Duke of York, brother of King Charles II.

They also introduced racially discriminatory legislation to force Khoikhoi and other so-called "free" blacks to work for as little as possible. (British Colonialism, n.p.a)

Also, Sierra Leone was assigned to British Empire. During colonization the country constituted a major source for the Europeans' slave trade until the British initiated a campaign against slavery in the 1760s and sent freed African slaves to the country to establish a "province of Freedom" under British protectorate. By the use of "indirect rule" the colonizers leveraged respect for their laws in return for British tolerance for local customs. (cf. ISS Africa, (n.d.), n.p.a).

The British colonial rule was characterized by an overall harsh behaviour by colonizers. The British Colonial Office in London made all the decisions concerning the colonies. The British also preferred ethnic societies with very hierarchical systems like their own; they recruited members of these ethnicities into the colonial military. (Africa: British colonies, n.p.a) The British administration was mainly characterized by a policy called "indirect rule". This indirect rule consisted in a clear division between the administrative sphere of the British colonial government and the local authorities. The first was in charge of the general resource management, while the second was tasked with liaising between colonial officers and native authorities. Each territorial entity governed itself via its original chiefs and institutions, whose authority derived from consuetudinary law. Indigenous authorities had large freedom of action, under the sole – heavy – condition of following the central colonial government disposition in the matter of administrative efficiency.

Under this general policy, different British colonies ended in having a heterogeneous system of local government. However, we can distinguish three main categories of colonial government:

- government of "dependencies", where the presence of European communities was large and native authorities were not established (South Africa, Southern Rhodesia, Kenya);
- hierarchic governments, where native population was more organized and outnumbered Europeans. Here the administrative hierarchy was mainly composed by native authorities;
- territories in which local societies were considered as lacking any form of government system, being only organized around a family- or clan-based system (so-called "backward tribes").

The "native authorities" system was originally developed by Lord Lugard, inspired by the structure of the Sokoto Caliphate, a theocratic and bureaucratized state located in present-day northern Nigeria. The colonial government that decided to establish a native authority was always looking for the cooperation with local chiefs: only when this was not possible, the colonial government had to individuate and nominate individuals for the role of local authority.

This system was based on fixed territorial division: this was very difficult to achieve, since that local communities followed different divisions and hierarchies often not linked with the British perception of territorial divisions. On such basis, the British went to create "artificial" territorial divisions, not following the existing relations among local populations: they even went to create the role of "paramount chiefs", supposedly in charge of such artificial administrative divisions. The term "multiple dependencies" was used to identify colonial territories administered by British governors supported by legislative councils.

The native authorities system showed all of its weakness by the time of the decolonization: it caused a radical change of the local power system, unbalancing the power relations among indigenous groups and creating room for increasing tensions as the colonial power faded.

2.4.4. Belgian Empire

Before the Berlin Conference, the Belgian king Leopold II urged his government to follow other European powers on the African continent; not receiving government support, the King decided to finance exploration missions by himself[19]. The explorers established treaties with several chiefs in the central African region (almost the whole Congo region), which guaranteed profitable economic concessions. Differently from the colonial empires of other powers, Belgian colonies originated more as a sort of "property" of the King, who aimed at obtaining overseas possessions for prestige and to create monopolies in the extraction and trade of specific commodities in order to spur Belgian economy. The Association Internationale du Congo (AIC) became the main instrument of the King's influence in the Congo territory, used later to monopolize trade in materials like ivory and rubber. (Sanderson, 1985, p.126-129)

King Leopold's AIC was not a real state; did it have neither a proper administration nor military force: it could have easily being overrun by competitors for central Africa- the French or British. Anyway, the positions of these two empires did not allow for a direct invasion. This competition, which even involved the Portuguese empire, was eventually resolved with the Berlin Conference, where the territory of Congo was assigned to King Leopold II. The structure of the AIC was transferred to the new Congo Free State, while the original AIC was terminated.

Leopold II did not care much about terms he had agreed in the Berlin Conference. Just a few years later Leopold II created a Force Publique, with the responsibility of ensuring the proper execution of his policies and rule. This Force Publique was Leopold's colonial army who had to maintain political stability in this territory, by eliminating

---

[19] See note 1 and 2.

resistance movements by any force. Moreover, it was responsible for defending the Belgian colonial territory from external forces, like the neighbouring French and German armies. (Schimmer, 2009, par.1-6)

In the late 19th century, Leopold broke several terms of the Berlin Conference. He created win-win situations for himself and Belgian companies, by providing them land to exploit in the Congo Free State and in return receiving 50% of their profits. The victims of these activities were the indigenous tribes, which were often expropriated of their lands and forced to work for Belgians.

In 1908, the control over the Congo Free State was transferred from Leopold II to the Belgian empire. At that time the Congo territory was of high economic importance for the Belgian empire, because of the high trading volumes of goods, such as rubber and ivory. Therefore the Belgians further supported the free flow of goods in their territory to promote for even more capitalism-driven companies. Even though the Belgian government decided to return some of the expropriated land to the indigenous Africans in the beginning of the 20th century, it soon established a poll tax, which had to be paid by Africans to make this Belgian colony more profitable.

The Belgian government also established a more efficient colonial administration. It created a colonial government, which dealt with issues concerning the Congo Free State territory and even assigned a colonial minister, who had the power to propose new policies to the colonial council (situated in Brussels). The administrators, which were primarily military officers, were partly replaced by civilians. The Belgians also applied the French concept of dividing its whole colony into several provinces. Therefore, the Congo Free State was divided into four provinces, which were governed by vice-governor-generals. (Jewsiewicki, 1986, p.460-472)

2.4.5. German Empire

In the second half of the 19th century also the German empire got increasingly involved in the colonization process on the African continent. The Germans wanted to stay competitive with other European empires, which already possessed territory in parts of Africa.

German foreign policy of the colonial era was dubbed Weltpolitik (lit. "world policy"): it aimed to transformation of Germany in a global power from being "just" a regional power by increasing the country's revenues, prestige and military power via the acquisition of colonies and the development of the navy, next to a more aggressive stance in diplomacy. Weltpolitik is considered as a strong break from the earlier policy stance, the "Realpolitik".

Educated German emigration and increased public interest in the Africa eventually led the German government to enter the competition for Africa, hoping that its citizens would rather migrate to its African colonies instead of other European empires. (Perras, 2004, p.31-46)

At the Berlin Conference, the Germans were assigned four colonies located on very different edges of Africa. In the south they were assigned German South-West Africa, in the east they possessed German East Africa and in the west- Cameroon and Togo. As the interest in colonies was shallow, they did not pay much attention to issues like the colonial economy and administration. The German position was to keep the indigenous officials in place and do not interfere their affairs until the German sovereignty and interests are threatened. The German government did not send much administration staff and did not provide a sufficient budget to build a proper administrative system in its colonies. Only small consulates were installed in order to assist and protect German traders and to administer certain parts of the colonies.

Due to the increasing complexity of administrative tasks in Africa, the German government established a more efficient system. Adapted system allowed them to exercise a direct control in all their colonies, except Togo, where the Germans still relied on African officials and soldiers. As a result each colony was headed by a governor, who was not only responsible for representative purposes and issues related to the specific colony, but also had to act as commander-in-chief of the police and military forces. The colonial territories were divided into districts, where local officials dealt with issues related to their districts, including the district police forces. Moreover district councils consisted of both, German officials and settlers. They were not powerful, but they had a notable influence to Berlin. The new administrative system improved the ability to exercise German rule on the African continent. However, it was still lacking in strength and resources.

Due to increasing complexity and uprising rebellions the German government established a colonial ministry in 1907. This action shifted a power from the colonial authorities back to officials in Berlin, but administrative structure was not experiencing a notable change. Direct political rule was increased by assigning more troops to the specific colonies. Nevertheless, the administrative changes were varying among the four German colonies. In some colonies a governor's chief assistant was assigned, who was responsible for dealing with administrative issues, such as medical care and agriculture, in order to exculpate the governor from some tasks. While in German East Africa, indigenous people were educated and trained in governmental areas, in order to reduce German administrative staff, by assigning official positions to these educated natives. A very fragile issue under the new administration was the treatment of Africa indigenous people, since the African were only treated as subject and were part of a special legislation, which only applied to them and allowed for punishment, detention and exercising the death penalty. (Gann & Duignan, 1977, Stanford University Press)

2.4.6. Italian Empire

Italy had an influential position in northern Africa for centuries, due to its strategic geographical location in the Mediterranean Sea, but it only got actively involved the colonization of Africa in the late 19th century after the process of national unification was concluded in 1861.

The newly-formed Italian kingdom was the last European power without an African colony. The need for colonies of Italy derived from both socio-economic demands and prestige related demands. Regarding the earlier, it should be remembered that Italian authorities thought that colonies could help the overpopulation problem in the south of the country; also, they thought that newfound resources could boost the national economy, making it more competitive in order to face internal post-unification challenges and improve its international position in respect of "stronger" neighbours.

Initially, Italy intended to establish a colony in Tunisia, due to its strategic position and proximity with the Italian territory; however, this plan was foiled by France in 1881, which abruptly took control of the area. Interestingly, this action pushed Italy towards the alliance with Germany and Austria (formalized one year later).

The first Italian territory on the African continent was the Bay of Assab, an important trading position located in Western Eritrea "unofficially" bought by the Italian government via the Rubattino Shipping Company; in 1882, the government formalized its official control on the bay by buying it from the shipping company.

Afterwards, the Italians shifted their focus to other areas of Eritrea and Ethiopia, which possessed huge areas of agricultural land. (Ahmida, 1994, p.103-105) One of the most notorious early attempts of expansion via military forces made by Italy ended in the infamous defeat of Dogali in 1887, where the Italian army was stopped by the Ethiopian Ras Aula Engida. After the death of the Negus Neghesti (literally, "the king of kings") John IV, Italy managed to successfully expand its territories in the area, also thanks to various agreements concluded with local lords who rivalled with John IV in 1889 – with Menelik being one of the most relevant at the time.

The strongest "wave" of Italian colonization in the horn of Africa took place under the Fascist regime, culminated with the conquest of Addis Ababa in 1936 after initial diplomatic negotiations in the late '20s. It should be noted that military and repression operations from Italian army and authorities often used weapons prohibited by the Geneva Convention as poisonous gases.

The territories of Ethiopia, Eritrea, Somalia and Libya where all united under the denomination of Eastern Italian Africa ("Africa Orientale Italiana" or AOI); AOI was disbanded in 1941 after the defeat of Italy in World War II.

The Italian government divided this colony into several districts controlled by Italian officials, in order to facilitate its administration.

Many Italian farmers migrated to Eritrea to improve their living situation, and the Italian government granted concession of agricultural land to Italian settlers. Moreover, the Italians separated different agricultural areas. For example, the Ethiopian highlands were mainly used to assure the supply of food to the Eritrean population, while the Ethiopian lowlands were mostly used for the cultivation of export products. Italian government also invested in improvement of the Eritrean infrastructure. The Italian empire also focused on the recruitment of Eritrean men to support the Italian army in battles for Libya and Somalia. (Adi et al., 2005, p.489-490)

In relation with these points, it should be noted the weight of Fascist ideology on the Italian strongest colonialist effort. The call for an Italian "empire" was made in order to satisfy still unanswered prestige-related needs of the post WW I early period; plus, the conquest of territories in another continent was seen as part of the "historical mission" of Fascism, consisting in reuniting the territories of Italy and Africa under the flag of Rome in remembrance of the ancient Roman Empire.

The conquest of Libya was one of the main objectives of the Italian, especially the territory of Tripolitania in the north of Libya. The Italians had been in a constant trading relation with Libya already for many centuries, but in the late 19th century this commercial interest developed into a strong political interest. Invasion of Libya took place in 1911. Italians faced a strong Libyan resistance. Nevertheless, the Italians reached an agreement with Libya, which consisted of many concessions. Italians had to permit that Libya would be self-regulated and autonomous during World War I. With the end of WWI, the Italian government started reconsidering these concessions and decided to terminate them and bring Libya under its control. Finally, in 1923 the Italian army successfully occupied Tripolitania. In 1932 the Italian government eventually managed to control the whole Libyan territory, after they had crushed almost all resistance movements. (Ahmida, 1994, p.106-107)

2.5. Decolonization of Africa

Due to the nature of colonialism and its progressive shift towards imperialist policies, among native ("colonized") peoples always fermented a feeling of opposition against foreign powers. This sentiment soon developed into a series of resistance movements (with a very variable degree of organization and institutionalization) and localized rebellions[20].

The end of World War I not only marked a serious shift in international relations and more than relevant modifications of European geography, but also a series of changes in the colonial policy.

---

[20] Notably, among the most notorious rebellions of the post-Berlin Conference period, there are the Herero Wars in German South-West Africa (1904-1907) and the Maji-Maji Rebellion in German East Africa (1905-1907).

Under the economic point of view, war demands for raw materials (and related services) created new stakeholders and internationally pushed towards inflation, consequently creating social problems in the lower classes and diffused unrest. The development of a native middle-class in the colonies translated in the creation of a new group of people with their own needs and demands; also, this led to a new wave of racism and social tensions.

Under the ideological point of view, the rise of nationalism in Europe involved also communities around the world, thus exacerbating the resentment against colonizers. Furthermore, the rise of Marxism and of the Soviet Union further pushed towards an anti-colonial sentiment, identifying foreign oppression as an expression of capitalism.

After the end of WWI, many African groups realized that the Europeans were vulnerable. Map 3 illustrates the political division of the European continent after the WWI. After WWI, many pro-African associations (e.g., East African Association[21]) were established and even more anti-colonial movements emerged all over the African continent. The nationalist and anti-colonial movements gained much support in the 1920s; during the Great Depression, the demonstrations against colonial rule got louder, due to the collapse of prices for goods, primarily exported from Africa. The working and the living conditions of Africans got worse, as they got increasingly forced to work without any tangible improvements of their living conditions. As a result many armed nationalist movements started to fight the European powers, but were still unable to repel them properly and manage to gain independence. (Adi et al., 2005, p.266-267)

---

[21] Founded in 1921 by the Kenyan politician Harry Thuku (1895-1970), the East African Association was Nairobi's first large political association. It advocated freedom and independence from colonial powers and missions, representing interests of local African stakeholders.

2.5.1. West Africa

The Western part of the African continent was mainly dominated by the French empire. The African natives did not want to fight the Europeans in terms of eliminating their colonial systems, like the North Africans. The population in this area rather desired a reform of the current administrative system. Especially the educated natives noticed the need for a change of the racialist policy of European powers. Moreover, they wanted to stop the recruitment of Africans to fight and die for the European armies in the First World War. Therefore, the indigenous people demonstrated and fight against inequality between natives and European settlers and against their poor living situation.

2.5.2. East Africa

In East Africa the relationship between African natives and the Europeans was more problematic than in West Africa. This was especially because the political movements in West Africa were consisting primarily of educated natives, while in East Africa the broad mass was demonstrating against European rule. Also in this area, the dissatisfaction over the compulsory recruitment of natives as well as the poor social situation of the population led to an increased nationalist activity. In the interwar period the demonstrating masses in East Africa, unlike West Africa were increasingly following religious leaders, which called for a colonial reform, instead of an elimination of the European administration. (Adu Boahen, 1990, p.270-285)

2.5.3. After the Second World War

During World War II, the European powers had to deploy their military forces in many different parts of the world. Their armies were weakened and that in turn gave the African population the chance to push for a change. The Africans gained support from the winners of the WW II – the United States of America and the Soviet Union –, which were also interested in the decolonization. Especially the United States wanted to combat racism in Africa and support the right of the Africans for self-determination. Many nationalist movements were founded and they received huge support from the native population and eventually managed to drive the European powers out of Africa, either by force or by agreement. Some European empires decided to peacefully withdraw from Africa by even providing the African natives with knowledge on how to lead a state, while other empires, like France fought wars against the African natives. Nevertheless, the result of such wars was mainly a peace agreement, which proclaimed the independence of the involved African state and included non-aggression clauses and mutual defence agreements. (Adi et al., 2005, p.267)

Chapter 3

INSTITUTIONALIZATION OF HISTORICAL EXPERIENCES IN AFRICA

The decolonization of Africa was a major turning point in the continent's history. While the European powers proclaimed a new era of racial equality and individual liberty, Africa found itself confronted with the legacy of its previous masters. However, with the decolonization process and the end of WWII, regional and supranational security systems became a necessity in order to maintain peace among the independent states and to avoid armed conflicts as results of unsettled border disputes. In addition to the inherited colonial conflicts, Africa became of major interest during the Cold War with the world's superpowers attempting to influence African politics and structures. (cf. Birmingham, 2003, pp. 1-5)

3.1. DEVELOPMENT OF BILATERAL SECURITY STRUCTURES

Proclaimed independence of African states scared Europeans that they will lose influence in the region. By the creation of institutions like the British Commonwealth of Nations, the Europeans kept a close political grip on African affairs and thereby could maintain close relations with their previous colonies even after releasing them into independence. In contrast, the Portuguese insisted on their status as a colonial power on the African continent, denying its overseas territories any kind of self-government. By following this strategy, Portugal missed the chance to find other ways of securing influence leading to the entire loss of relations to its former colonies, which by then had come under another nations' sphere of influence under those of the Soviet Union. (cf. ISS Africa, 1999, n.p.a)

After 1945, the confrontation between the United States and the Soviet Union also reached Africa. Taking advantage of the disruptive relation between Portugal and its former, the Soviet Union stepped in as their new partner providing some of them, mainly Angola, Mozambique, Guinea Bissau and Uganda, with military aid in order to be able to protect their gained independence. (cf. BBC, (n.d.), n.p.a)

3.1.1. China's Presence in Africa

Although this work exclusively deals with European and African security structures and their comparison, we will mention the bilateral ties between China and Africa as an exception, since all African bilateral ties are primarily with the former European colonial masters. In the 1950s and 1960s, China and Africa fought shoulder to shoulder in the historic struggle against imperialism, colonialism and hegemony, and worked side by side in the hard endeavour to revive their respective national economies. Common historical experiences have played important role in establishment of strong relationships between China and Africa. China has always attached importance to Africa, and to enhance its solidarity and cooperation with African countries has always been a key pillar in China's foreign policy. The relationship between China and Africa in recent years has been characterized by a more economic than ideological stance.[22] China's rapid development has provided the third-world countries with a new alternative to establish cooperation as China opens market. Africa has business interests to China, while China is also a huge and enormous market for African countries.

Chinese Premier Wen Jiabao in his speech at the 4th Ministerial Conference of Forum on China-Africa Cooperation approves also Africa's contribution to China:

> "[…] while Africa's tremendous effort in helping restore China's seat in the United Nations, the successful Beijing Olympic torch relay in Africa and Africa's generous donations to the victims of the Wenchuan earthquake in China give full expression to the friendship of the African people toward the Chinese people[…]."(Embassy of People's Republic of China in the Republic of South Africa, 2009)

Chinese Premier in the same speech said that China is ready to deepen practical cooperation with African countries in diverse areas and gives following proposals:

- strengthen strategic coordination to uphold common interests;
- meet the MDGs and improve the livelihood of the African people;
- enhance economic cooperation and trade to realize mutual benefit and win-win progress;
- promote people-to-people exchanges to solidify China-Africa friendship;

---

[22] This point needs specific attention. The success of China's penetration in the African continent is linked to the fact that Chinese operators introduced themselves to African partners as economic and trade partners, instead of focusing on a vague "ideological" basis focused on contrasts. It has managed to fully surpass a Cold War-like mind set in creating relationships with foreign countries.

- expand areas of cooperation and advance The Forum on China-Africa Cooperation (FOCAC) institutional building.

These proposals include (1) establishment of China-Africa partnership in addressing climate change, (2) enhancement of cooperation with Africa in science and technology, (3) help Africa build up financing capacity, (4) further opening up of China's market to African products, (5) enhancement of cooperation in agriculture, (6) deepening of cooperation in medical care and health, (7) enhancement of cooperation in human resources development and education and finally (8) expanse of people-to-people and cultural exchanges. (cf Embassy of People's Republic of China in the Republic of South Africa, 2009)

An interesting aspect of contemporary cooperation activities between China and Africa is that, differently from cooperation in the Cold-War era, Chinese institutions limit themselves to the promotion of economic activities instead of contextualizing it in a wider international political propaganda scheme.

3.1.1.1. *China and South Africa*

Relations between China and South Africa have enjoyed comprehensive and rapid development since the two important developing countries established diplomatic ties in 1998. The main goal is to realize the common development of both countries. China and South Africa have become important strategic partners by cooperating in international and regional affairs such as the global financial crisis and climate change. Besides mutual political trust, cooperation has increased in fields like economy and trade, culture, education, science and technology, health and tourism. China also now is the biggest export destination and the largest trade partner. Chinese enterprises have started business in African countries with a direct investment stock of 7.8 billion U.S. dollars. (cf. Embassy of People's Republic of China in the Republic of South Africa, 2009)

3.1.1.2. China and Sierra Leone

Sierra Leone records a very low performance on the Human Development Index and on the Human Poverty Index, following years of civil wars. China forged diplomatic ties with Sierra Leone on July 29, 1971. China supports economic construction of Sierra Leone through enhanced bilateral cooperation in agriculture, infrastructure, education, public health and resource exploration. China also collaborates with Sierra Leone in major issues including peacekeeping, poverty reduction and fighting against global challenges. So far, China had invested 33.9 million U.S. dollars in the country and helped build more than 30 projects including hydropower stations, a national stadium, hospitals and government buildings. (cf. Embassy of People's Republic of China in the Republic of South Africa, 2009)

3.1.1.3. China and Zimbabwe

Zimbabwe is among the biggest economies in the Southern African region. In last decades it has experienced political instability, which led to a decline in the economy and the country has become from being a manufacturer to being a consumer of finished products. One of the detrimental effects to this downturn is bottlenecks in the country's road network. Therefore China helps with equipment for transport and communication as well as agriculture and mining industries. Furthermore, China has contributed for the establishment of the Zimbabwe inclusive government. In addition, by establishing Care Action China provides support to Zimbabweans affected and infected by HIV, including orphans and the physically challenged. Due to the cooperation between these two countries, Zimbabwe's economy is growing at a time when most African nations are feeling the effects of the global financial crisis. (cf Embassy of People's Republic of China in the Republic of South Africa, 2009)

3.1.1.4. *China and Sudan*

China and Sudan established diplomatic ties on Feb. 4, 1959. The two countries had conducted sound economic cooperation, with bilateral trade standing at 8.2 billion U.S. dollars in 2008. China supports Sudan's economic development and social stability by collaborating in politics, economy and military affairs as well as in agriculture, energy and other areas. (cf Embassy of People's Republic of China in the Republic of South Africa, 2009)

3.1.1.5. *China and Djibouti*

Recently, China keeps strengthening its presence in Djibouti, both under the military and economic cooperation profiles. Starting from May 2015, when the Djiboutian President Ismail Omar Guelleh announced talks with the Asian "giant" regarding the establishment of a military base of theirs in his country. This will be the first example of a Chinese-operated permanent military base on the African continent. The early intent of the Chinese government in setting up such facility derived from the difficulty of resupplying during anti-piracy missions. In January 2016, after the November 2015 talks, new steps toward consensus have been made. However, Chinese projects in Djibouti are not limited to the military sphere: the latest step of security-related talks were anticipated by the signature of economic agreements, covering: the establishment of a free trade zone, an improved legal framework supporting Chinese banks operations in the country, and the empowerment of a transhipment hub for international Chinese trade.

3.2. Development of Multilateral Security Structures

After decolonization, there were attempts to create supranational organizations according to pre-colonial structures. However, those early international systems failed within few years, e.g., the East African Federation, the Ghana-Guinea-Mali Union and Senegambia. (cf. Herbst, 2000, p. 102) As pre-colonial structures were inappropriate, future African attempts for supranational cooperation were based on the nation states.

The increasingly bi-polar international system as well as the perceived South African nuclear threat provided a major security concern for the continent as a whole. Meanwhile the general preoccupation of military threat as the sole determinant of state security changed to the assumption that also state internal factors have to be considered when talking about regional security. Acknowledging this theory, the concept of security substantially widened in scope from the 1960s on incorporating now factors such as a country's economic environment, the socio-political state, the citizens' well-being as well as the environmental situation. The African states eventually started focusing on cooperative security structures in order to preserve their recently gained independence. (cf. Oyebade and Alao, 1998, pp. 1, 3-4)

3.3. The Concept of Cooperative Security

"There is need for simple but reliable structures for security cooperation that can stabilize relations, prevent spillover of conflicts, secure emerging common values and perhaps, lay the foundation for new security regimes. In the absence of effective crisis response structures, regional peacekeeping initiatives will continue to be ad hoc, poorly implemented and driven by the interest of the strongest in the region." (DFID Report, 2001)

The concept of cooperative security plays an essential role in the creation of efficient security architecture on the African continent. Considering the challenges of violent inter-state wars and the problems of complex political emergencies in Africa, regional organizations will continue to play a dominant role in resolving transnational problems as conflicts occurring in a certain area is only of interest of a specific regional organization (cf. Francis, 2006, p. 113).

Generally, Africa has found an effective framework for cooperative security based on the creation of regional organizations, which again work together if necessary in order to solve problems of greater dimension affecting several of them. The most important ones in Sub-Saharan Africa are ECOWAS; IGAD, SADC, ECCAS and EAC which are rather successful in pursuing their objectives. Certainly, the commitment of the organizations´ member states can differ according to its current head of state or government policy.

3.4. REGIONAL SECURITY ORGANIZATIONS IN AFRICA

As it has been mentioned before, security is often more effectively addressed on a regional level. Reasons for a common regional defence and security system:

- supranational threats to a nation´s security;
- decreasing suspicion and rivalry among an organization´s member states;
- increasing transparency of participating states´ military apparatuses and their defence systems;
- making national defence and security systems more cost effective;

- freeing capital for reallocation to address other, economic or humanitarian, problems.

Facing these advantages of cooperation in the security field, various regional security organizations have developed in the 1990s with almost all African states participating in one or more of them (cf. EASBRIG, (n.d.), n.p.a).

It is interesting to point out the fact that not only security and police/military oriented organizations delve into security-improving practices, but also regional economic communities and economic development-oriented bodies focus on peacekeeping activities. This can be related to the fact that security is perceived as a fundamental asset needed to promote enduring development under both the social and economic point of view.

3.4.1. Economic Community of West African States (ECOWAS)

ECOWAS was founded as a solely economic cooperation of Western African states in 1975. In 1978 as a response to the newly developed theories on the interrelation of a state´s economy and its security structures, it started also to cover economic, monetary and financial, social and cultural matters as well as security activities. Moreover, a defence assistance agreement has been signed in which any seizure of power by force of arms is being condemned. Because of region´s recent history, which was mainly marked by disastrous wars and humanitarian catastrophes, the organization shifted its emphasis from conflict resolution to conflict prevention and therefore created its own security and defence body; the ECOWAS Monitoring Group (ECOMOG) (cf. ISS Africa, (n.d.), n.p.a).

In case of conflict, the ECOMOG empowers a Mediation and Security Council consisting of a Committee of Ambassadors, a Committee of Ministers of Foreign Affairs, Defence and Internal Affairs and Security and a meeting of Heads of States of the member states. (ECOWAS) In case of armed conflicts in one of its member States, the ECOWAS may employ political as well as military interventions. Another innovation of the ECOWAS' system is its commitment to peacekeeping operations in situations, which might cause humanitarian disasters, pose a threat to security in the sub-regions or attempt overthrowing democratically elected governments. Considering these principles, ECOWAS has successfully deployed ECOMOG forces already in 1997 in Sierra Leone and in 1999 in Guinea Bissau (ibid).

Furthermore, in 2010 ECOWAS strengthened its commitment in peacekeeping activities with the ratification of the ECOWAS Conflict Prevention Framework (ECPF) and the consequent establishment of the ECOWAS Stand-by Force (ESF).

In addition, it should be remarked that ECOWAS managed to show a strong and increasing commitment in the maintaining of peace in the region while cooperating with international bodies with initiatives like the Sahel Strategy Document, realized with the African Union and the United Nations.

3.4.2. Intergovernmental Authority on Development (IGAD)

Founded by seven East African countries in 1996 the IGAD replaced the Intergovernmental Authority on Drought and Development, created in 1986, in order to expand cooperation among the member states and to adopt the organization's structure to its new fields of operations (cf. IGAD, 2007, n.p.a).

IGAD´s Peace and Security Division deals with all issues related to peace and security in the region and is organized in three main division programs; Conflict Prevention, Management and Resolution (CPMR), Political Affairs and Humanitarian Affairs. The CPMR is involved in Post-Agreement activities following up peace initiatives of Sudan and Somalia conflicts to actually secure that the agreed on decisions will be followed and enforced. Encouraged and supported by the UN and the AU, IGAD also established a standby brigade, the EASBRIG, which additionally highlights the organization´s commitment towards the management of conflicts in the region (cf. Francis, 2006, pp. 222-225).

Moreover, the security division also coordinates the activities of two other IGAD security institutions; the IGAD Capacity Building Programme Against Terrorism (ICPAT) and the Early Warning and Early Response Mechanism secretariat (CEWARN) (ibid).

More than any other African regional organization, the IGAD focuses on humanitarian affairs since this part of the African continent is constantly suffering from devastating conflicts and natural disasters that results in masses of refugees and displaced persons spread all over the region. Thus, the organization has created programs like the Regional Food Security and Risk Management Program (REFORM), the Regional Disaster Fund, the Risk Management of Bird Flu and various refugee programs to respond more rapidly and efficiently to these problems.

3.4.3. Southern African Development Security (SADC)

Preceded by the SADCC, the SADC was founded in 1992 in Windhoek as an organization aiming at the development, economic growth, alleviate poverty and enhance the standard and quality of life of the peoples of Southern Africa. One of the main reasons for restructuring the organization in 1992 was the desire to create a common security organ which was then realized in form of the SADC Organ on Politics, Defence and Security Cooperation (OPDSC) (cf. ISS, (n.d.), n.p.a).

The OPDSC is structured into three divisions, which all have to report to the regularly held Heads of State and Government Summit (HoSG). These three divisions are made up of the Inter - State Defence and Security Committee (ISDSC), the Ministerial Committee of the Organ (MCO) and finally of the Interstate, Politics and Diplomacy Committee (ISPDC). The ISDSC is further subdivided into three sub committees, namely, a defence subcommittee, a public security subcommittee, which is mainly dealing with immigration issues, and a state security subcommittee (cf. ISS, (n.d.), n.p.a).

Given the complexity of security and the factors affecting peace, SADC's generous subdivision of tasks and responsibilities aims at the provision of a highly sophisticated structural organization, almost unique among African regional organizations.

3.4.4. Economic Community of Central African States (ECCAS)

Deriving from the 1983 established Customs and Economic Union of Central Africa, the ECCAS had been inactive, due to conflicts among the member states, until 1999 when the members again confirmed the importance of ECCAS and agreed on restructuring the organization especially adopting its peace and security related activities. Already in 1994 the central African states signed a pact of non-aggression, however, just in 1999 they created an organization for the promotion, maintenance and consolidation of peace in the region; the Council for Peace and Security in Central Africa (COPAX) (cf. African Union, (n.d.), n.p.a.).

This newly created organ is made up of the Central African early-warning system (MARAC), which generates data for the early detection of crisis, the Defence and Security Commission (CDS), which is a meeting of chiefs of staff of national armies, police commanders and gendarmerie forces and the Central African multinational force (FOMAC), which is a non-permanent military force consisting of contingents from all member states (ibid).

3.4.5. East African Community (EAC)

EAC has been established in 1999 by the East African states Kenya, Uganda, Tanzania, Rwanda and Burundi. It was created as a regional intergovernmental cooperation aiming to collaborate for their mutual benefit in fields such as politics, economy, social issues and security. Recognizing peace and security as the ultimate prerequisites for the EAC's success, the organization is creating a framework and structures dealing with security problems which are, however, hampered by the absence of clear strategic direction on critical areas of cooperation (cf. EAC Portal, (n.d.), n.p.a).

Nevertheless, the need for peace in the region caused the deepening of cooperation triggering the implementation of collective security strategies that cover collaboration on cross border crimes, drug trafficking, terrorism, money laundering and other crimes.

3.5. THE CONCEPT OF COLLECTIVE SECURITY AND DEFENCE

In Africa the concept of collective security was hardly feasible to introduce as states would always put national interest higher that collective ones. Therefore, until the African Union was established,

Africa was mostly relying on the United Nations as an outside power disposing of the force to resolve conflicts. Hence, it has not been possible to establish an organization solely dealing with security and defence issues such as the NATO in Europe. Instead, a pan African and various regional organizations have evolved which are all following their own, respectively shared, security and defence policy. However, due to deficits faced by regional organizations in their peacekeeping actions, several Western governments and the United Nations are providing peacekeeping support until African institutions may take over these tasks. Some of these Western forces are the UN African Crisis Response Initiative, the French Reinforcement of African Peacekeeping Capacities and the British International Military Assistance Training Team (cf. Francis, 2006, pp. 98-99). Contrary to Africa´s approach to security, Europe has started right after WWII to create almost exclusively collective security structures being institutionalized through the NATO. However, while NATO has been the most effective institution in terms of military interventions, the EU (as following a cooperative approach) has done relatively better in post-conflict prevention (cf. Bajrektarevic, 2008, p 18).

3.5.1. The Organization of African Unity

Almost a century of colonization by foreign powers and the fear of neo-colonialism through the two ideological opponents United States and Soviet Union finally provided the African people with a common historical experience out of which they were able to formulate common future objectives. In order to achieve those, the African states established an organization in which these desires should be institutionalized; the Organization of African Unity.

In May 1963 in Addis Ababa, the OAU was founded by the leaders of 32 independent African nations endeavoured to establish a peace, security and conflict resolution architecture aimed at safeguarding and consolidating independence as well as the sovereignty and territorial integrity of the states, and to fight against neo-colonialism in all of its forms (OAU, 1963, p. 39).

Strategies to pursue these desires were formulated, four of them being the most important ones due to their long term relevance:

- determined members to ensure independency of still colonized countries
- policy of non-involvement in the East-West ideological conflict
- the endorsement of "non-interference" in the "internal affairs" of other African countries (which limited ability to create further internal security structures)
- maintenance of member states borders, drawn by Europeans and that rarely reflect real ethnic, social or linguistic boundaries (cf. Oyebade and Alao, 1998, pp. 5-7), (Werbner/Ranger, 1996, p. 148).

However, the lack of an executive body of the organization, which could have enforced the agreed on strategies and objectives, permitted its members to interpret the provisions differently without fearing any consequences. Furthermore, the OAU's peacekeeping operations proofed to be rather reactive only responding to emergency situations instead of preventing them.

By the end of the Cold War, a new era for Africa also was marked, as the block nations lost their interest in the continent and accordingly stopped providing it with arms, technology and know-how. This development, combined with the disruptive campaigns of the African states themselves led to a repeated marginalization of the continent excluding it from international politics. This sudden worsening of Sub-Saharan Africa's economic situation resulted in increasing political instability and eventually in war. The OAU was thus forced to find out about the correlation of these events and had to rethink its approach to peace.

Finally, the organization concluded in the Declaration on the Political and Socio-economic Situation in Africa in June 1990 in Kampala the redefinition of security and recognized the interrelation of peace, security, socio-economic development, democratization, human rights and good governance at national and regional levels as the key to peace and security in Africa (Francis, 2006, pp. 118-123).

As a response to the modified principles, the OAU established a Mechanism for Conflict Prevention, Management and Resolution (MCPMR), specific security divisions within the OAU secretariat and a Peace Fund, which should finance the work of this mechanism. Moreover, this new system should anticipate close cooperation with the UN and other African organizations in order to respond more rapidly to emerging crisis (cf. Francis, 2006, p. 123).

3.5.2. The African Union

In 2002, the OAU was replaced by the African Union (AU), which

> "[...] was founded on the promotion of closer integration between existing African states. The Constitutive Act spoke in language of democracy and respect for cultural rights, and placed particular emphasis on conflict resolution [...]." (Nugent, 2004, p.105)

The AU introduced the collective participation of peacekeeping operations in crisis regions. Together with UN peacekeeping missions it is the goal to bring peace and stability to war torn zones which shall further make space for negotiations and a peaceful resolution of conflicts. The AMISOM mission in Somalia is an example for such an initiative. Somalia had to struggle with a civil war for about 16 years. With this Peace Support Operation the African Union is trying to secure peace. It is their goal to support the inhabitants with humanitarian aid and to install a safe and stable environment for reconstruction and development of new institutions. This operation is also preparatory work in order to prepare Somalia for the transition to the UN.

3.5.2.1. The Vision of the AU

> "[...] principal organization for the promotion of accelerated socio-economic integration [...], which will lead to greater unity and solidarity between African countries and peoples.
> [...] common vision of a united and strong Africa and on the need to build a partnership between governments and all segments of civil society, in particular women, youth and the private sector, in order to strengthen solidarity and cohesion amongst the peoples of Africa.
> [...] focuses on the promotion of peace, security and stability on the continent [...]." (African Union, 2009, par. 7)

The main decision making body of the African Union is the Assembly, which consists of the Heads of States and governments of the member states. There is a meeting at least once a year; however there can be extraordinary meetings if necessary. The chairmanship is held by one member country for one year after being elected by the other member states. The main tasks of the Assembly include, but are not limited on the determination of the main policies of the Union. The decisions are taken by consensus or by two-thirds majorities.

The Executive Council is a subordinate organ to the Assembly. It consists of the Ministers of Foreign Affairs or other authorities designated by the respective government of the member state. The Council meets twice a year on a regular basis. The main task of this organ is to implement the policies, which were decided upon the Assembly. The decisions are taken by consent or by a two-third majority.

The commission consists of the chairperson and 8 commissioners (deputies and secretaries not included). This organ represents the Union and defends its interest. Furthermore, it is responsible for monitoring, analysing, planning and implementing policies and reforms for the AU member states.

The Permanent Representatives Committee is another major pillar in the organizational structure of the AU. The PRC consists of the assigned representative of the member states and it concentrates on the preparation of the work for the Executive Councils.

Besides these main decision-making bodies, the AU also consists of the following:

- Peace and Security Council (PSC)
- Pan-African Parliament
- Economic, Social and Cultural Council (ECOSOCC)
- The Court of Justice
- The Specialized Technical Committee
- The African Central Bank
- The African Monetary Fund
- The African Investment Bank

Most of these institutions, however, have consultative duties only. Another focus of the activities of AU bodies lies on the monitoring, implementation and reporting of the projects and policies, which have been decided upon the Assemblies or Executive Councils.

3.5.3. Organization for Islamic Conference

The OIC, established in 1969, is the second largest intergovernmental organizations after the United Nations. The OIC is a very important forum for the Islamic African countries, which make up half of the OIC's member countries.

The organization has consultative and cooperative relations to the UN and other inter-governmental organizations in order to protect the vital interests of the Muslims. They are working together closely in order to increase economic integration and stability.

The main decision making body of the OIC is the Islamic Summit, which consists of the Kings and Head of State and Government of the members states. The summit has the supreme authority as they meet once every three years. The Council of Foreign Ministers meets once a year and is setting the framework in order to realize the objectives which have been decided upon the Islamic Summit. The General Secretariat is the executive body of the organization: it works on the implementation of the decisions of the Islamic Summit and the Council of Foreign Ministers.

The OIC as the United Nations is an important part of African security structures. Although the organization is only focusing on Islamic countries it, however, tries to increase peace and stability with the mean of political and economic development. By putting a focus on the religious diversity, the organization creates the possibility of increasing friction between Islamic and not Islamic countries in Africa.

3.5.4. Extractive Industry Transparency Initiative

Founded in 2003, this initiative is still in its early phases. EITI defines itself as *"a global standard to promote the open and accountable management of oil gas and mineral resources"* (Rustad, 2017).

Regarding its goals, *"The Extractive Industries Transparency Initiative (EITI) aims to strengthen governance by improving transparency and accountability in the extractive sector."* (Extractive Industry Transparency Initiative, 2009, par. 1)

The aims of EITI are linked to the frequent occurrence – not limited to African countries – of the so-called phenomenon of the "Resource curse[23]" or "Paradox of plenty", which argues that *"[...] that abundant natural resources do not produce the expected blessings but turn out to be a "curse"[...]"* (Basedau and Mehler, 2005, p.12).

The mostly unexpected inflow of large amounts of money is a danger for any country without a stable government. State leaders are often blinded by the huge amounts of money flowing in from natural resources. Thus, they focus more fiercely on the extraction of these resources and forget to diversify their economic structure; as a result, investments in other economic branches are neglected. The heavy export-oriented approach increases the dependency towards the trends of global markets, ultimately weakening national economy.

Furthermore, the "curse" is often the trigger for corruption, inequality and unrest that leads to corrupt politicians and middlemen who gain excessively from the trade with natural resources. At the same time these resource rich countries become important suppliers for developed countries. Instability and deteriorating conditions often become matters of national security for other countries like USA, EU or China. External influences additionally contribute to internal instability[24].

Hence, *"The EITI is a coalition of governments, companies, civil society groups, investors and international organizations [...]"* (cf Extractive Industry Transparency Initiative, 2009) who want to increase

---

[23] The definition "resource curse" has been initially proposed by Richard Auty in the book "Sustaining Development in Mineral Economies: The Resource Curse Thesis" (Routledge, 1993), in which was outlined the problem of mineral-rich countries which actually were made poorer by the mismanagement of natural resources.

[24] For further insight on the subject and the application of theory to a different geographical context, see Ahrend, R. "How to Sustain Growth in a Resource Based Economy? The Main Concepts and Their Application to the Russian Case", OECD 2006.

transparency and sustainable management of the venues from natural resources.

EITI currently counts 51 member countries, of which about a half is located in the African continent.

3.5.5. Kimberley Process

This initiative has the same targets as the previously mentioned Extractive Industry Transparency Initiative. The Kimberley process *"is a joint governments, industry and civil society initiative to stem the flow of conflict diamonds – rough diamonds used by rebel movements to finance wars against legitimate governments."* (cf Extractive Industry Transparency Initiative, 2009)

This approach aims to stop the indirect foreign funding of armed conflicts in Africa. Due to the "resources curse" African countries had to deal with foreign influence. As long as there is no functioning state and legal system corrupt local politicians, warlords and multinational companies try to exploit the African poverty in order to gain access to natural resources (gold and diamonds). The trade with these stones *"has fuelled decades of devastating conflicts in countries such as Angola, Cote d'Ivoire, the Democratic Republic of the Congo and Sierra Leone"* (cf Extractive Industry Transparency Initiative, 2009), hence the name "blood diamonds".

The Kimberly process certification scheme puts certain requirements on its member states in order to guarantee that the traded stones are conflict-free. Participating countries have to implement specific administrational institutions and have to provide statistical data as well as transparency.

3.6. COLLABORATING SECURITY INSTITUTIONS

As traditional state-centric national security concerns have narrow focus, the new comprehension of peace has developed additional areas of focus, which can not only be dealt by governmental organizations or which they are only able to address to a limited extend. Hence, various non-governmental organizations have developed on the African continent addressing security factors that would have been otherwise waived or neglected. Moreover, such institutions often act as intermediaries between organizations in order to align their strategies and coordinate their activities in the various African regions.

3.6.1. Centre for Democracy & Development (CDD)

Founded in the United Kingdom in 1997, the CDD is an independent non-profit research, advocacy and capacity building organization aiming at the mobilization of resources for the democratization process in West Africa. Concerned about the security aspect of democracy, the organization promotes peace and human security in collaboration with regional institutions and the civil society. Moreover, the CDD deals with the further institutionalization of early warning and response to conflicts in West Africa and the development of strategic coherence of organizations operating in the region for conflict prevention in West Africa (cf. CDD West Africa, (n.d.), n.p.a).

3.6.2. Institute for Security Studies (ISS)

Originally established in 1991 as the Institute for Defence Policy, the ISS is today a leading African human security research institution. As definition of the term security has changed, the organization is also concerned with human rights, good governance, community security, justice, refugee movements, food security and various other aspects of security. Following these goals, the institute is also engaged on a collaborative basis with state institutions, like the four regional security organizations mentioned before. Therefore, the ISS networks with governmental and intergovernmental partners as well as civil society organizations; additionally, it supports these organizations during the implementation process of their projects not only with know-how and data but also with technical assistance (cf. ISS Africa, (n.d.), n.p.a).

3.6.3. New Partnership for Africa's Development

Founded by the OAU in 2001, the NEPAD was created to develop an integrated socio-economic development framework for the continent. It focuses on four key factors: the prevention, management and resolution of conflicts, peace-making, peacekeeping and peace enforcement, post conflict rehabilitation and reconstruction and combating the illicit proliferation of arms, light weapons and landmines. However, in order to substantially achieve its security objectives, the organization follows a holistic approach focusing on human security issues, e.g., civil-military relations, public safety, crime prevention and access to justice (cf. Ball, (n.d.), p. 19).

3.7. INTERNATIONAL ORGANIZATIONS

Despite strong efforts by the African nations and organizations, international organizations are still playing a vital role regarding the development of peace and security structures and the underlying economic development on the African continent. The most essential organization operating in Africa are certainly the United Nations with their various institutions, commissions and programs.

3.7.1. United Nations

Since its founding, the United Nations is a key player in African politics and development. The organizations goal in Africa is to maintain peace and improve living conditions by economic and social development. To achieve this goal the UN has implemented various regional commissions and organizations.

All these organizations support the African states in:

- Promoting economic growth
- Reduce poverty
- Regional integration
- Strengthen institutions and capacity development.

3.7.1.1. United Nations Economic Commission for Africa (UNECA)

The UN Economic Commission for Africa (UN ECA) has been established in 1958 by ECOSOC as one of the United Nations' five regional commission.

The regional arm of the UN in Africa supports its 54 Member States in *"promoting Regional Integration in support of the African Union vision and priorities."* and *"meeting Africa's special needs and emerging global challenges."* (United Nations Economic Commission for Africa, 2009, par. 4)

The tasks basically consist of research and analysis (monitoring) of politics as well as support in economic development and focuses on following thematic areas:

- Macroeconomic Policy
- Regional Integration and Trade
- Social Development
- Natural Resources
- Innovation and Technology
- Gender
- Governance.

Furthermore, UN ECA provides technical advisory services to intergovernmental institutions and organizations, as well as governments. It also develops assistance programmes. Additionally, UN ECA provides capacity development support and specialized regional advisory services to member states in priority areas as follows:

- Promotion of industrialization
- Design and implementation of macroeconomic policy
- Design and articulation of development planning
- Supporting mineral resources contract negotiations
- Promoting the proper management of natural resources for Africa's transformation.

In the framework of UN ECA-related bodies, the African IDEP (Institute for Economic Development and Planning) needs to be mentioned. IDEP is a pan-African institution established by the United Nations' General Assembly in 1962, with the primary task of supporting the countries that recently obtained independence. IDEP operates as a sub-programme of UNECA, with a functional position in the overall Commission's action and approach. The main activities of the Institute take place in two main programmes: the Capacity Development and Training Programme, focusing on education and offering a series of short courses and master degrees; and the Research

Support Programme, aiming to help policy-makers with original research on specific critical topics in the areas of development.

IDEP is managed by a governing council composed of 12 members, of which 11 are African Ministers of Finance, Economic Development and/or Planning, while the twelfth is the UNECA Executive Secretary or the UN Under Secretary-General. While Senegal, being the host country of IDEP, holds a permanent seat, the other ministerial representatives are drawn with criteria of 2 per sub-region of Africa on a rotational basis.

The Council is the main decision-making organ of the Institute; it is supported in its action by the Technical Advisory Committee and the Management, Programmes and Administrative Units.

3.7.1.2. United Nations Peace Keeping

The UN peacekeeping missions are an instrument established by the UN Security Council in 1948 and has been used a total of 63 times around the world by the UN in order to intervene in local conflicts and thereby maintain peace and stability. Although this UN instrument was initially aimed at dealing with inter-state conflicts, the UN peacekeeping missions have been increasingly applied to intra-state conflicts and civil wars. Despite the focus on military, most peacekeeping missions today include administrative, economic, police and legal, de-miner, electoral observing, human rights monitoring and other operations (cf. Peacekeeping, (n.d.), n.p.a.).

Since its foundation in 1948, peace keeping missions had to intervene already nineteen times on the African continent including conflicts in Ethiopia, Eritrea, Rwanda, Uganda, Angola, Burundi, Côte d'Ivoire, Congo, Central African Republic, Mozambique, Sierra Leone, Somalia and other African states.

In recent times, seven UN missions have operated in Africa; the United Nations Mission in the Central African Republic and Chad (MINURCAT), the African Union-United Nations Hybrid Operation in

Darfur (UNAMID), the United Nations Mission in the Sudan (UNMIS), the United Nations Operation in Côte d'Ivoire (UNOCI), the United Nations Organization Mission in the Democratic Republic of the Congo (MONUC), United Nations Mission in Libearia (UNIMIL), and the United Nations Mission for the Referendum in Western Sahara (MINURSO).

3.7.1.3. United Nations Development Program (UNDP) in Africa

Founded in 1965, the UNDP is a global development network aiming at connecting countries to knowledge, experience and resources in order to improve their populations´ quality of living. Today, the UNDP is present in 45 Sub-Saharan African countries and is there collaborating with regional institutions and other UN agencies and partners in order to accelerate progress towards the Millennium Development Goals. These Millennium Development Goals were agreed on by world leaders and are supposed to be achieved until 2015 and focus on dealing with the challenges in the fields of Democratic Governance, Poverty Reduction, Crisis Prevention and Recovery, Environment and Energy and HIV/AIDS.

In each of the 45 African country offices, the UNDP Resident Representative also serves as a coordinator for all development activities of the United Nations system as a whole.

3.7.1.4. G-77

The Group of 77 (G77), which was founded in 1964, is the largest intergovernmental organization of developing states in the United Nations. G-77 incorporates 130 member countries deriving from Africa, Asia, the Caribbean and Latin America but has retained its original name due to its historical significance.

The chairmanship, which rotates every year on a regional basis, is the highest political body within the organization of the G77. The chairman acts as spokesperson and is responsible for the coordination of the Group's action. The South summit is the supreme decision making body. It is convened once in every five years. Additionally there also exists an annual meeting of the ministers of foreign affairs. The ministers of the G77 member countries usually meet at the beginning of the regular session of the General Assembly of the United Nations in New York.

By working together, the developing countries from the different continents try to have a stronger say in the international negotiations especially in context of economic policies and international trade (trade barriers and substitutions for agriculture of industrialized nations). Especially for Africa this organization can be used as a tool to enhance cooperation and integration. Common goals on the international stage force the African countries to work together in order to be successful.

3.7.1.5. UN Convention on the Law of the Sea

The Third World United Nations Conference on the Law of the Sea (UNCLOS 3) is one of the greatest successes of the United Nations in its history. After about 9 years of negotiations almost all African states (119 countries) signed the treaty on the law of the sea in 1982. Before that, international law was mainly decided by western powers. The outcome of the convention itself is remarkable as well. It constitutes of 320 articles, 9 annexes and there is no right for reservation. This means that the treaty is an "all-or-nothing" package.

The treaty itself was an unprecedented attempt of the international community (including underdeveloped countries) in order to regulate all aspects of the resources of the sea and uses of the ocean. Stability should be increased with the definition of navigational rights, territorial sea limits, economic jurisdiction, legal status of resources on the seabed beyond the limits of national jurisdiction, passage of ships through narrow straits, conservation and management of living marine resources, protection of the marine environment the introduction of a marine research regime and an additional binding procedure for the settlement of disputes between States.

Today the Convention of the Law of the Sea is getting more important again because of the high level of piracy in some African coastal states. Especially Somalia is known for its density of pirates who are attacking civilian ships on international waters (Elias, 1988, p.266).

3.8. European Legacy

The post-colonial period was very difficult to handle for the African natives, because most European powers left within short time, without providing sufficient knowledge and assistance to the new self-administering African nation-states. That caused not only internal political conflicts but also many external disputes between neighbouring nation-states. Due to the fact that the European powers did not unite numerous different tribes to form one colonial entity, the problem of dealing with those differences emerged when they left. The European colonies handled as nation-states still contained tribes of many different languages, customs and cultures. Because the European powers were treating some tribes better than others an internal conflict among those tribes appeared. Moreover, the borders between the colonies, which were put in place by the Europeans, often separated similar tribes, which were later even driven into rivalry under colonial rule. New nation-states had to face also several internal problems. Because throughout European dominance the African natives never experienced any kind of democracy, they simply adopted this attitude in their new self-regulative system. The European way of having only one party in place, which exercised full powers, was used by African politicians to establish dictatorships or in some regions even military rule. (Oduor Ndege, 2005, p.276)

3.8.1. Portuguese

Portugal was one of the first European Powers to claim African territory as colony and had successfully been defending its claims since the 15th century. Already in 1497, the entire African continent came under Portugal´s sphere of influence thanks to the Treaty of Tordesillas[25] in which Spain and Portugal divided the territories of the New World between them. Nevertheless, despite having been the first power to enter and the last one to leave the African continent, it was unable to maintain its influence after decolonization. Portugal attempted postponing the decolonization process for as long as possible not abandoning its claim on its African territories until it entirely lost control over them as a result of the lost so called Portuguese Colonial War. As a result, Portugal had also neglected the possibility to find other ways for linking the now independent states to the home country (Birmingham, 2003). In 1996 the Community of Portuguese Language Countries was founded in order to promote the Portuguese language and culture in its 11 member countries. Attempts to extend its field of operation to economic and security matters remained relatively insignificant although the community could serve as an intermediate in conflicts in Sao Tome and Guinea-Bissau and assisted in taking economic and democratic reforms (cf. CPLP, (n.d.), n.p.a).

The economic performance of former Portuguese colonies until present day varied greatly. For example, although Portuguese former colony Cape Verde has hardly any natural resources and is located about 600 kilometres west of the African mainland, today it is one of the relatively bright spots in Africa with its well managed economy and generally uncorrupted bureaucracy. The economy is mainly privatized and open to foreign investors. Cape Verde seeks cooperative relations

---

[25] Signed on 7 June 1494 in the city of Tordesillas (Castile, Spain), substantially "diveded" the non-European world in a sort of duopoly between the Spanish and the Portuguese Empire along the north-south meridien at 1770km west to the Cape Verde islands.

with all countries and maintains multilateral agreements with countries like the United States, Russia or Portugal.

Contrary, Angola having been colonized by Portugal from the 15th century on, the country not only inherited the Portuguese language but also a rigid and backwards form of bureaucracy that also had a negative influence on post-colonial administrations. (cf. Chabal, 2008, p. 3)

3.8.2. French

The area in Africa that was and still is influenced by France is referred to as the francophone area. France as colonial power was mainly active in the western part of the African continent. Starting from Morocco and Algeria, French influence stretched to the south (Togo and Cote d'Ivoire) and east (Chad).

French as the *lingua franca* is a sign of the strong influence of the former colonial power in these geographic regions. Henceforth external politics of the new African states (after independence) was and still is oriented towards France. Although of the independence of its former colonies, France continued in pursuing its interests in these areas (Franc Zone). The use of international companies, organizations and bilateral treaties with the African governments should maintain this influence. This form of international politics was often regarded as the new form of colonization.

After independence, African governments were seeking for external military assistance, as they could not maintain control over their territories. France intervened strongly by maintaining military camps within former colonies. It additionally presented itself as a main player in internal affairs as governmental parties could rise or fall with the support of the French. Today, as in the past, France is a strategic key player in African affairs. Its long relationship with the African people and its national interests (in natural resources) however make it difficult to examine whether France is a contributor to stability or not. This can be seen only on a case-by-case analysis.

Also, France manages its foreign aid policy and action via two State-controlled entities: FDA[26] and PROPARCO[27]. The first manages financing/funding actions from State to State, while the other operates mainly with the private sector.

Additionally, it is useful to spend some words on the so-called concept of "Françafrique" and its practical implications in both politics and diplomacy. The term "Françafrique" derives from the expression "France-Afrique", used for the first time in 1955 by Felix Houphouet-Boigny - at the time President of Ivory Coast - to define the strong relation still linking former French colonies to France. Initially, the term bore a positive meaning but in more recent years - in 1998 - this neologism was used again with a negative meaning by François Xavier Verschave[28] in his book entitled *"La Françafrique, le plus long scandale de la République"* (Françafrique – the longest scandal of the Republic). In this work, Mr. Verschave uses this term to describe the system of "underground" relations kept running among the French government and various African authorities and institutions, in order to keep stable countries supporting France and vice versa. Verschave also defined Françafrique as "the secret criminality in the upper echelons of French politics and economy, where a kind of underground Republic is hidden from view". He also - ironically - suggested that the tern could be read as *"France à Fric"*, which roughly translates to "France for cash".

---

[26] French Agency for Development or AFD, Agence Française pour le Développement. Established in 1998, it is the successor entity of the Caisse Centrale de la France Libre (Central Fund for Free France), active from 1941.
[27] PROPARCO (Promotion et Participation pour la Coopération économique, literally Promotion and Participation for Economic Cooperation) is an agency partly under control of AFD and funded by private investors from both developed and developing countries. It mainly aims to promote private investment in activities in less developed countries.
[28] François Xavier Verschave (1945-2005) was a French economist and journalist.

The reasons behind the establishment of this system mainly related to three perspectives:

- economic perspective: the system guaranteed France the access to commodities and natural resources (gold, uranium, etc.);
- diplomatic-strategic perspective: counter a potential "communist invasion" of the African continent while, at the same time, coordinate the opposition towards the excessive influence of the USA in the area;
- political perspective: organizing the "occult" funding of French political parties by African ruling elite parties.

The African countries considered part of the Françafrique are the following:

- in West Africa: Senegal, Ivory Coast, Burkina Faso, Togo, Benin, Niger, Mali;
- in Central Africa: Congo (Brazzaville), Gabon, Chad, CAR, Cameroon;
- in the Horn of Africa and in the Indian Ocean: Comoro Island, Madagascar, Djibouti.

Institutional instruments for putting into practice the "Françafrique system" are the African cell of the Elysée, which manages French foreign policy in Africa independently from the Ministry of Foreign Affairs.

When they managed to achieve independence from France, various African countries signed defence agreements with their former "homeland".

For example, in 1961 France, Ivory Coast, Niger and Dahomey[29] signed an agreement about the establishment of French military forces in these countries. For defence needs, these countries sell their strategic commodities (hydrocarbons, lithium, and uranium) to France and, in case of specific defence-related demands, limit or interdict the sale of these same products to other countries.

Next to the fact that France has the second most extensive consular network worldwide (right after the United States), it is important to note that Françafrique manoeuvres more via unofficial networks and emissaries operating to support French interests. These actors cover or covered political or intelligence positions, while others are mercenaries or managers in private companies active in strategic sectors (as energy and such).

3.8.2.1. La Francophonie - The International Organisation of La Francophonie

The term "la francophonie" and therefore also the International Organisation of La Francophonie relates to all the french speaking countries with the mutual usage of the same language. All of these countries have been colonised from the former French Empire. The language together with the respect to its universal values and beliefs build the two cornerstones of the institution. The geographically incoherent Francophonie, which already struggels with the appeal of inconsistency and fragility, identifies itself as culturally and linguistically diverse and furthermore let understand the new approach of individualisation and common identification in a time of globalising conditions. (La Francophonie, 2009)

The OIF, founded in 1970, has the mission (which is defined in a Strategic Framework for ten years, from 2005 to 2014) to embody the

---

[29] The kingdom of Dahomey roughly occupied the area of present-day Benin. It lasted from 1600 circa to 1894, when it was conquered by France. It regained independence in 1960 and changed its name to Benin in 1975.

active solidarity of all member states by cooperation and multilateralism. Like many other important international organizations it, furthermore, emphasizes on the necessity to establish and develop democracy, human rights and peace as well as to the promotion of the French language and to find solutions through education and training. The OIF tries to fulfil its part as "the voice of diversity" by organizing political relations and acting as co-operator between the largest linguistic zones which share the usage of the French language. The institution implies over 870 million people, with more than 200 million French speakers and represents one third of the members of the United Nations. The OIF cooperates with many international organisations, such as the European Union as well as the African Union. The International Organization of the Francophonie has 70 member states or governments consisting of 56 member and 14 observer states (30 out of the 53 member states of the African Union and 15 of the 27 member states of the European Union are members of the OIF). (La Francophonie, 2009)

There are three main political decision making instances. The highest political power are the Conferences with representatives of the governments or Head of States, commonly called Summits; uniting every two years for further discussions on goals and principles which have been signed by the member states. Moreover, the second and third instances are Ministerial Conference of La Francophonie (CMF) and the Permanent Council of Francophonie (CPF). The Parliamentary Assembly, with the support of four special operators, namely the Academic Agency of La Francophonie (AUF), TV5Monde the television channel, the International Association of Francophone Mayors (AIMF) and The Senghor University of Alexandria and the two permanent ministerial conferences, the Conference of Ministers of Education (CONFEMEN) and the Conference of Ministers of Youth and Sports (CONFEJES) are responsible for implementing programs and agreements decided during the summits. (La Francophonie, 2009)

3.8.3. British

Even after decolonization, although far from being peaceful, the British kept close ties to their former colonies by the use of institutions like the Commonwealth of Nations.

The former British colony namely South Africa is one of the economically most successful and politically most stable ones on the continent, despite continuous clashing of different ethnic groups. However, although apartheid has been abolished in 1991, racism remains a serious threat to the country's internal security. Apartheid having been the country's political policy of strict segregation of ethnic groups, putting all South Africans into racial categories, for more than four decades had also major influence on the nation's security policy. The fear of revenge of other black African countries for degrading its black population strengthened South Africa's striving for nuclear weapons which eventually also guaranteed its military dominance in the region (cf. Global Security Org, (n.d.), n.p.a).

Mostly because of radical racial policy, the country was pushed towards continental isolation and international marginalization. However, the end of apartheid also marked the end of isolation. South Africa began re-establishing bilateral ties with African states and other countries that had previously announced trade sanctions against it. These agreements provide for training, exchange of military intelligence, military cooperation and joint exercises. South Africa has also re-establish its multilateral cooperation by re-entering organizations such as the Commonwealth of Nations and the International Community, the IAEA, the Southern African Development Community (SADC).

Nonetheless, despite its current putative stability, South Africa faces new internal and external security threats including organised crime, drug trafficking, a vast wealth disparity, large scale HIV infection within its population and heavy involvement in the continent's trouble spots in terms of security forces and peacekeeping deployments potentially also threatening the country's own stability (cf. PRLog Free Press Release, 2008, n.p.a).

In 1963, also, Kenya became independent and one year later turned into a republic and joined the Commonwealth. During the first decade after independence, Kenya's economic performance was better than most in Africa. The rate of economic growth was among the highest on the continent. From that time on Kenya's growth rate declined continuously and today Kenya has one of Africa's worst performing economies despite increasing growth rates in the last view years. Kenya is a member of several multilateral co-operations such as the UN, IMF, WTO or the AU. Aside from ties with advanced economies and donors, Kenya is active within regional trade blocs such as COMESA and the EAC, a partnership of Kenya, Uganda, and Tanzania with the ultimate aim to create a common market of the three states modelled on the European Union (Library of Congress, 2007, p. 13).

Currently Kenya has security problems with its neighbours (Somalia, Uganda and Sudan), and problems that relate to the country's escalating levels of violence and crime. One year after independence Kenya signed a formal defence treaty with the United Kingdom by which London offers measures of military assistance and, in return, Britain was permitted to use military training facilities in Kenya. In early December 2001, a deal was struck between Nairobi, Washington and London whereby Kenya gave his consent for US and British military forces to use Kenya as a base for action against Somalia, where the US alleges Osama bin Laden's al-Qaeda network and other militant groups to have active cells. Both London and Washington are believed to have promised President Moi (the Kenyan president at that time) additional (unspecified) security equipment during discussions between British and US military officials with their Kenyan counterparts in Nairobi. (cf. ISS Africa (n.d.), n.p.a)

Since the last presidential elections in 2007, widespread unrests have been increasing and are deteriorating the country's reputation for stability. Despite its own politically unstable situation, Kenya has been acting as a mediator in conflicts in Somalia and Sudan (cf. Library of Congress, 2007, p. 19).

Nevertheless, another former colony -Sierra Leone- is still facing severe security issues as most of its conflicts are taking place on a regional rather than on a national basis and thus, can´t be declared ended as long as there is instability in the country´s very neighbouring countries, mainly caused by rebels and demobilized but still armed fighters hiding in Guinea, Liberia and Sierra Leone's own hinterland. However, formerly being highly dependent on foreign security forces, the country´s police and military are today receiving training and equipment from the Commonwealth Training Team and from an International Military Advisory and Training Team (IMATT). Although the country is gaining stability, its relationships to international organizations such as the UN, EU, ECOWAS and the Commonwealth of Nations and their member states is still essential for the countries security. Sierra Leone alone still would not be able to address all the factors influencing it (cf. ECOWAS, (n.d.), n.p.a).

3.8.3.1. The Commonwealth of Nations

The modern Commonwealth of Nations was established in 1949. In the 'London Declaration', it was agreed all member countries would be "freely and equally associated." The first member to be ruled by an African majority was Ghana, which joined in 1957. Sharing a common history and language the Commonwealth of Nations supports democracy and cooperation in all of its 54 member states. Beyond the ties of history, language and institutions, it is the association's values, which unite its members: democracy, freedom, peace, the rule of law and opportunity for all. (cf. Commonwealth, (n.d.), n.p.a.)

3.8.4. Belgian

In comparison with other colonial powers in Africa, Belgium did less to prepare its overseas subjects for political independence, investing little in education and training, and extracted the riches of its colonies at enormous human cost.

The Belgian colonialists were active in Congo, which is located in the centre of Sub-Saharan Africa. Belgian influence was no contributor to regional stability: weak institution building and empowerment of inequality (support of ethical minorities over the majority) were key points which lead to heavy turmoil in the Congo region after gaining independence.

> "Congo is home to a paradox: it is one of the most mineral-rich countries in the world and at the same time one of the poorest and most conflict-ridden" (cf Basedau and Mehler, 2005, p.145)

The prompt departure of the Belgian empire from the Congo is an example on how dangerous and irresponsible it can be to dismiss a country into independence very unprepared under the institutional profile. It underlines the importance of a stable state apparatus with strong legal institutions in case a country has a great wealth in natural resources.

Today Belgian influence happens mainly with the presence of national companies (oil, gas and diamonds). Additionally Belgium is a contributor to humanitarian missions under the UN or the EU flag.

3.8.5. German

The short time of German colonization left notable marks in Africa. Germany kept its African colonies from the Berlin Conference period until World War I, when they were seized by enemy forces and then confiscated after Germany lost the war. The German colonial period was characterized by strong repression of local communities[30], as well as by the establishment of concentration camps where locals were subject to forced experimentations[31].

On a completely opposite trend, present-day Germany's foreign policy is working in Africa as a positive force. Development cooperation between Germany and for example Cameroon and Namibia is aiming to improve conditions in the *"[...] fields of health and HIV/AIDS, decentralization, participatory development and good governance [...]."* (German Federal Ministry for Economic Cooperation and Development, 2009, par. 6) Furthermore, Germany's military as part of the EU or UN is also actively participating in peace keeping operations across the African continent (e.g., Chad).

3.8.6. Italian

Italy's focus is oriented towards the horn of Africa. Italy with bilateral means and also as member of the EU is working towards peace processes in the Eastern hemisphere of Africa. Somalia, Ethiopia/Eritrea and Sudan are the major points of influence.

Development cooperation as well as peacekeeping missions have the goal in increasing regional stability and development. (Italian Ministry of Foreign Affairs, 2009)

In particular, Italy is a strong contributor of military apparatus for UN peacekeeping missions.

---

[30] The worst of these repression acts was the Herero and Nama genocide (1904-1907, during the Herero Wars period). It is considered one the first acts of genocide of the 20th century; it has been estimated that casualties ranged from 24000 to 100000 Herero and 10000 Nama circa.

[31] Experimentations mainly involved eugenics and sterilization. Eugen Fischer (1894-1967), one of the lead scientists performing such inhuman acts, strongly influenced Nazi thought and engaged in providing "scientific" bases for the anti-semitic Nuremberg Laws.

Recently, Italy showed renewed interest for Western Africa. In February 2016, Prime Minister Matteo Renzi visited three countries in the area to promote bi- and multilateral relations between them and Italy. Furthermore, the Italian government signed with Senegal the PADESS (*Programma di Appoggio allo Sviluppo Economico e Sociale Senegal*, Senegal Programme for Supporting Economic and Social Development) agreement.

Chapter 4

INSTITUTIONALIZATION OF HISTORICAL EXPERIENCES IN EUROPE

The history of the European security structure can be seen as a successive development, a reciprocating movement between a unified and a separated Europe with a multiplicity of self-acting nations. With its cultural superiority and highly developed imperial structure, the Roman Empire established a unified European security order on a large scale for the first time in European history. The fall of Rome and countless wars in medieval and modern times led to decentralized political control and a decrease in a centralized balance-of-power order in the European continent. (cf. Buzan and Waever, 2003, pp. 345-347) After the Second World War, Europe tried to stabilise and empower the role of Europe with different organisations and policies to build up a strong defence program and taking measures on different divisions, such as human rights, environment and politics. Europe started alliances and organisations, also with overseas partners in order to fulfil the best outcome on security measures.

4.1. Raison d'État, Peace of Westphalia and the Balance of Power

After the fall of the Roman Empire it came to a separation of powers and the concept of unity collapsed. In the 16th century the Italian diplomat and politician Machiavelli created the reason of state (raison d'état) to unify all the Italian states in order to "rescue" Italy from its dependency on other states and to protect its own existence. The newly established European states adopted this principle together with the balance of power. Acting upon the reason of state means that in case of a conflict the interests of a state override all other objects of legal protection and interests and, if necessary, to breach the norms of the legal system in order to keep a state capable of acting (cf. Paulsen, 1996, pp. 12-13).

The Peace of Westphalia brought an end to the Thirty Years' War in Europe. It lasted from 1618 to 1648 and almost every major nation in Europe was involved. A wave of nationalism was created and the meaning of a nation state was redefined. Leo Gross describes the Westphalian nation state as the following: "A Westphalian nation-state has two main characteristics: a specific area of land which is considered part of the nation, called territoriality, and a ruling structure that has the ultimate power to rule over the nation without yielding to any external agency."(cf. Gordon, 2008, pp. 3-4).

The treaty was accepted by all of Europe. Thus, it was ensured that no single monarch would be able to dominate Europe such as the Habsburgs had prior to the start of the Thirty Years' War. The first step towards a multilateral Europe was made and it is still strongly associated with the model of the nation state and today scientists refer to the modern model of nations as "Westphalian sovereignty" (cf. Asch, 1997, p. 149).

Within the European balance of power, Great Britain played the role of the "balancer," or "holder of balance." It was not permanently identified with the policies of any European nation, and would throw its weight once at one side, at another time on another side, guided largely by one consideration—the maintenance of the balance (Britannica, (n.d.), n.p.a).

This phenomenon happened several times during the 18th century as for example during the War of Austrian Succession (1740-48). It was fought between France and its allies against Austria. Britain joined the war and fought on the side of Austria because it feared that France could become the dominant power in Europe and hence saw its commercial and colonial empire at risk. Its naval supremacy and its virtual immunity from foreign invasion enabled Great Britain to perform this function, which made the European balance of power both flexible and stable (Britannica, (n.d.), n.p.a).

After the Napoleonic Wars the general policy of Europe was changed. At the Congress of Vienna in 1815 three permanent principles to direct Europe were established:

- to incorporate her force, simplify her action, and organize it according to the wants and convenience of nations;
- to separate her means of defence into two grand divisions, in opposition to the two Powers which menaced Europe at the time (namely, Great Britain and Russia);
- to extend general civilization in its interests with the interests of Europe. Due to the principles defined at the Congress of Vienna the longest period of peace in Europe was possible (cf. De Pradt, 1816, pp. 168-169).

This peaceful era lead to a growth of population in Europe (the population more than doubled in the 19th century), industrialization (due to a great development of technology), social developments (e.g., legal foundation and growing cities due to industrial factories and towns), rising nationalism and colonization. Meanwhile Realpolitik came into being to maintain "the balance of power operating within a multiple-state system" (cf. Wayman and Diel, 1994, p. 185).

Thus, the term Realpolitik can be referred to as a formal association of states for the use (or non-use) of military force, intended for either the security or the aggrandizement of their members, against specific other states, whether or not these other states are explicitly identified. In the 1890s the German chancellor Bismarck wove a network of defence alliances following this Realpolitik approach to preventing war in central Europe by ensuring that any aggressor would confront multiple adversaries (Wayman/Diel, 1994, pp. 187-189).

At the beginning of the 20th century the European balance of power assumed a new form, one which was characterized by bipolarity as the major European powers formed themselves into two hostile alliances. Because of its bipolar character after 1907, the system encouraged a fear in both coalitions in losing allies to the opposite camp. This was a significant and ominous development. A feature of the 19th century balance of power system up to that point had been the fact that the great powers did not conceive of it as operating in 'zero –sum' terms, where one side could only benefit at the expense of the other. As the nineteenth century progressed the scope for reciprocal great power compensation diminished, and a zero-sum mentality did emerge after 1900 (cf. Sheehan, 1996, pp. 135-136).

4.2. THE CONCEPT OF COLLECTIVE SECURITY AND THE POST-VERSAILLES ORDER

By applying collective security system states attempt to prevent or stop wars. The core idea is that the governments of all states would join together to prevent any of their number from using coercion to gain advantage, especially conquering another. Thus, no government could with impunity undertake forceful policies that would fundamentally disturb peace and security. Any attempt would, by definition, be treated by all governments as if it were an attack on each of them (Weiss, 1993, pp. 3-4).

In 1918, the president of the United States, Woodrow Wilson, hoped to create together with the great powers of Europe a new world order to replace the balance of power system, which had allegedly failed in 1914. With the Wilson's 14 points, which were based on the concept of selective security, they tried to establish a community of power, not organized rivalries, but an organized common peace. The League of Nations was established as a system of collective security (Sheehan, 1996, p. 153).

In 1919, the order of post-war Europe was defined by the treaty of Versailles. The terms of this treaty viewed Germany as the main instigator of the war and demanded the demilitarization of the country; also, with the "war guilt" clause, the treaty forced Germany to accept complete responsibility for initiating the conflict. The harsh conditions imposed by the treaty of Versailles created the conditions for the birth of radical right-winged parties in Germany, such as Hitler's NSDAP; the critical economic conditions of Germany gave room to the the rhetoric and propaganda of such political movements for obtaining mainstream acceptance during the 1920s and early 1930s. Hence, the treaty on the one hand ended WWI but on the other established some of the conditions for the outbreak of one of the most vicious dictatorship in European history, as well as was one of the main reasons for the outbreak of the World War II (USHMM, (n.d.), n.p.a).

The most innovative point of the treaty of Versailles was the creation of the League of Nations (cf. Boemeke et al., 1998, p. 507). The treaty was based on collective security and was the first of its kind. However, the league was unable to realize the ideal of collective security as a number of major powers remained outside its membership when it was founded (United States in particular) posing one of the main reasons for its downfall (cf. Sheehan, 1996, pp. 159-160).

4.2.1. United Nations

After failing to prevent WWII, the League of Nations as an organization failed and collapsed. The name "United Nations" was first used in the "Declaration by United Nations" of 1 January 1942, during the Second World War, when representatives of 26 nations pledged their governments to continue fighting together against the Axis Powers and was meant to be an improvement of the League of Nations. In 1945, representatives of 50 countries met in San Francisco at the United Nations Conference on International Organization to draw up the United Nations Charter. Those delegates deliberated on the basis of proposals worked out by the representatives of China, the Soviet Union, the United Kingdom and the United States. The Charter was signed on 26 June 1945 by the representatives of the 50 countries. (UN, (n.d.), n.p.a)

According to the Charter, the purposes of the UN are:

1. To maintain international peace and security, and to that end: to take effective collective measures for the prevention and removal of threats to the peace, and for the suppression of acts of aggression or other breaches of the peace, and to bring about by peaceful means, and in conformity with the principles of justice and international law, adjustment or settlement of international disputes or situations which might lead to a breach of the peace;
2. To develop friendly relations among nations based on respect for the principle of equal rights and self-determination of peoples, and to take other appropriate measures to strengthen universal peace;
3. To achieve international co-operation in solving international problems of an economic, social, cultural, or humanitarian character, and in promoting and encouraging respect for human

rights and for fundamental freedoms for all without distinction as to race, sex, language, or religion; and
4. To be a centre for harmonizing the actions of nations in the attainment of these common ends (UN, (n.d.), n.p.a).

Today, the work of the United Nations reaches every corner of the globe. Although best known for peacekeeping, peace building, conflict prevention and humanitarian assistance, there are many other ways the United Nations and its System (specialized agencies, funds and program) affect our lives and make the world a better place. Due to its unique international character, and the powers vested in its founding Charter, the Organization can take action on a wide range of issues, and provide a forum for its 192 Member States to express their views, through the General Assembly, the Security Council, the Economic and Social Council and other bodies and committees (cf. UN, (n.d.), n.p.a).

4.3. THE POST-WORLD WAR II INTERNATIONAL ORDER

After the end of WWII John Maynard Keynes was convinced that his principle of "cooperative multilateralism" was the answer to overcome the nationalisms and antagonisms that had ultimately led to the horrors of WWII. Keynes was also convinced that multilateral institutions were necessary in order to facilitate and enshrine cooperation on equal basis between countries. In the Conference of Bretton Woods in 1944, two more global institutions were created. Firstly, the IMF with the goal to provide assistance in emergencies and secondly the International Bank for Reconstruction and Development (IBRD, better known as World Bank) in order to provide loans for reconstruction and development. Initially a third institution, the International Trade Organization (ITO) with the goal to negotiate and enforce trade agreements, was foreseen, but negotiations proved more complex and therefore only a part of the initially planned organization was established with the General Agreement on Tariffs and Trade (GATT) that was later improved and transformed into the World Trade Organization (WTO) (cf. Schekulin, 2007, pp. 15-16).

4.4. THE CONCEPT OF COLLECTIVE DEFENCE, NATO AND WARSAW PACT

Collective defence refers to participation in the defence of Europe as in the event of aggression. The signatory states are required to provide assistance for the restoration of security. Hence, two treaties were signed, the treaty of Brussels and the North Atlantic Treaty. The treaty of Brussels was signed in 1948 by France, the United Kingdom, Belgium, the Netherlands and Luxembourg. It was amended in 1954 by the Paris Agreements establishing the Western European Union (WEU). The North Atlantic Treaty Organization (NATO) was founded in Washington in 1949 by ten Western European countries, the United States and Canada. Both treaties imply a principle of mutual assistance in the event of an armed attack against any of contracting parties (cf. Europa, (n.d.), n.p.a).

NATO was established to prevent the USSR (and Germany, to a lesser extent) from dominating Europe. NATO, in fact, originally was a purely defensive alliance to protect Western Europe and was not able or willing to project its power anywhere else (cf. Duignan, 2000, pp. 2-3).

In 1955, the Warsaw Pact was founded as a counterpart of NATO after West Germany joined the Treaty organization. The Pact was superimposed on the network of bilateral treaties of mutual assistance that had linked the Soviet Union and its dependent states in Eastern Europe with one another (cf. Mastny and Byrne, 2005, pp. 1-2).

In the late 1990, by the time the Soviet Empire was already faltering, the NATO and the Warsaw Pact members signed an unprecedented Treaty on Conventional Armed Forces in Europe (CFE). The treaty imposed equal ceilings on nonnuclear weapons located between the Atlantic Ocean and the Ural Mountains as well as limitations on each side regarding military equipment and restrictions on where these forces where to be deployed (cf. Duignan, 2000, p. 50).

After the fall of the Soviet military block the role of the NATO as an organization and its operations were redefined. The key aspects involved are the recognition of a European defence identity, the strengthening of the European component of the transatlantic security system, and the prospect of the eastward enlargement of NATO. This will be accompanied by a deepening of NATO's relations with third countries through partnerships for peace and the North Atlantic Cooperation Council. A major challenge in this connection is that of establishing a sound, stable and sustainable partnership with Russia and Ukraine (cf. Europa, (n.d.), n.p.a).

In relation with this topic, it is important to underline NATO's engagement with strategic counterparts with the Partnership for Peace (PfP) programme, initially proposed during the Travemunde meeting (Germany, October 1993) and formally constituted in January 1994 during the NATO summit in Bruxelles. NATO itself defines the PfP as *"a programme of practical bilateral cooperation between individual Euro-Atlantic partner countries and NATO. It allows partners to build up an individual relationship with NATO, choosing their own priorities for cooperation."* [32]

The current members are 22, being they mainly former Soviet states or European countries not yet fully adhering to NATO[33]; 12 former PfP members fully joined NATO between 1999 and 2009[34].

---

[32] As stated on NATO official website, http://www.nato.int/cps/en/natolive/topics_50349.htm
[33] Current members include (as of 2012): Armenia, Azerbaijan, Belarus, Georgia, Kazakhstan, Kyrgyzstan, Moldova, Russia, Tajikstan, Turkmenistan, Ukraine, Uzbekistan, Bosnia, Republic of Macedonia, Montenegro, Serbia, Austria, Finland, Ireland, Malta, Sweden, and Switzerland.

The PfP Programme embraces all of the fields of activity of NATO, including "defence-related work, defence reform, defence policy and planning, civil-military relations, education and training, military-to-military cooperation and exercises, civil emergency planning and disaster response, and cooperation on science and environmental issues."

The role of NATO expanded also outside of European borders, gaining a relevant support role in peacekeeping/peacebuilding and police actions in various regions of Africa led by international forces and/or the US forces.

In relation with the action of the United States in global security and counter-terrorism, it is important to underline the role of AFRICOM (United States African Command, also known as USAFRICOM).

Washington's military operations are – from 2008 – under control of AFRICOM and UCC (Unified Combatant Command), which are in charge of the entire African continent excluding Egypt (which falls under the direct jurisdiction of the US Department of Defence).

Before the establishment of AFRICOM, the security in Africa was under the responsibility of three different Commands: the European Command, responsible for West Africa; the Central Command, active in Eastern Africa; the Pacific Command, in charge of the Indian Ocean area and islands nearby. This setting, with responsibilities territorially divided among three different Commands, was inefficient in responding at the growing challenge of facing well-organized enemy militias: logistics operations and the chain of command were overall slow and, additionally, the various difficulties raised from operating in a complex

---

[34] Regarding this point, specifically in relation with the joining of NATO by the Baltic States (Estonia, Latvia, and Lithuania), NATO expansion towards Eastern Europe has been criticized by various analysts, especially from post-Yeltsin Russia. Criticism points out that, during the final years of the Cold War era, Soviet and US Heads of State informally agreed on the suppression of both NATO and the Warsaw Pact or that, at least, NATO would not expand soon towards Soviet territory.

territory – being these difficulties of both socio-political nature and of a merely geographic/topographic nature – did not leave room for this setting to operate correctly, with the United States incapable of applying a coherent and well-defined strategy for Africa.

On such bases, as analysed by the US War College in 2000, American authorities reflected on the idea of unified command, needed in order to ease the operations management by starting from what was happening in the Sahelian-Saharan belt.

The first effort in this sense was made in 2000, when the Congress approved circa 500 million dollars of funds for the Trans-Saharan Counterterrorism Initiative (TSCTI) – an enhanced version of the Pan-Sahelian Initiative (2002-2004). The TSTCI is a multi-agency operation not limited to specifically military actions, whose military component was active in the wider framework of the Operation Enduring Freedom – Trans-Sahara. TSTCI has been designed to stay operational six years, trying to involve a higher number of countries when compared with its predecessor. Algeria, Chad, Mali, Niger, Senegal, Nigeria, Morocco and Mauritania were among its African partner countries.

The initiative's main objective consisted in the contrast of arms smuggling activities and drug trafficking, together with support activities to the training of local military forces.

As noted by certain analysts, the evolution of the activity of terrorist organizations in Africa has strong possibilities of being one of the determining factors of the United States' strategic planning in the area, together with other contingent factors as the Chinese expansion in Africa under the economic and the military profile.

In 2006, under the Bush presidency, US authorities launched the first study for the establishment of a new unified command for Africa. In February 2007, the Secretary of Defence Gates announced that the President initiated works for the creation of this new military command for Africa; the announcement was followed by the dispatch of high-level US military personnel to Stuttgart, with the objective of initiating the preparatory works towards the establishment of the renewed African command.

On September 28, 2007, the US government nominated General William Ward was nominated first commander of the unified command, AFRICOM. This new entity was granted complete independence; on October 1, 2008, it officially finalized the absorption of the existing commands for Africa based in Europe.

All but one of the main bases of AFRICOM are located outside of the African Territory. Among them, we remember:

- USARAF (United States Army Africa): located at the Ederle base near Vicenza (Italy). It hosts the land forces of the army;
- MARFORAF (Marine Corps Forces for Africa): USMC component based in Stuttgart (Germany);
- USAFE (United States Air Force in Europe): air force based in Ramstein (Germany). USAFE forces are available for sorties on the African territories.
- NAVEUR-NAVAF: US Navy forces deployed at the Naval Support Activity structures in Naples (Italy);
- SOCAFRICA: special forces available to AFRICOM, with headquarters in Kelley Barracks, Stuttgart-Mohringen (Germany).

Even if the United States support various military operations on the African territory, they have only one permanent military base on this continent: the Camp Lemonnier base in Djibouti (Eastern Africa).

The position of the Camp Lemonnier base is strategic for support activities to US (and allied) operations in the Gulf area. Camp Lemonnier hosts the Combined Joint Task Force – Horn of Africa (CJTF-HOA) of AFRICOM, originally established at Camp Lejeune in October 2002 and repositioned in the Horn of Africa on December 8, 2002.

CJTF – HOA operates under the 5th fleet of the US Navy. Its main task involves the training of troops originating from neighboring countries in the domain of counter-terrorism and counter-insurgency; additionally, CJTF – HOA is tasked with humanitarian activities (not limited to reconstruction of schools, clinics and medical facilities in countries sending troops for training).

Non-permanent US military bases in Africa are located in twelve countries: Mali, Burkina Faso, Niger, Nigeria, Chad, Central Africa Republic, Democratic Republic of Congo, South Sudan, Uganda, Ethiopia, Kenya and Somalia. Specifically, the US are present in Burkina Faso's capital Ouagadougou from 2007, with a base mainly used as a hub for the observation and espionage network established in the region in order to control the areas of Mali, Mauritania and Sahara for counter-terrorism purposes. In Ethiopia, the base of Arba Minch is a structure mainly maintained for the use of Reaper-class drones (mainly used for espionage and control purposes). In the Democratic Republic of Congo and in the Central African Republic (from 2013), US Troops support the local military in operations countering the Lord's Liberation Army activity: in both cases there is a limited deployment of troops, as in Camp Simba (Kenya) near the Somali border.

4.5. COOPERATIVE EUROPEAN SECURITY

Originally, Cooperative Security defines a cooperation of defence-oriented military forces, multinational coalitions, and service for international purposes. However, this definition has expanded and now also includes a country's perceptions of its economic and environmental security (Moodie, 2000, p. 3).

4.5.1. The Council of Europe (CoE)

Founded on 5 May 1949 by 10 countries[35], the Council of Europe seeks to develop throughout Europe common and democratic principles based on the European Convention on Human Rights and other reference texts on the protection of individuals. The Council of Europe, based in Strasbourg (France), now covers virtually the entire European continent, with its 47 member countries (CoE, (n.d.), n.p.a).

The primary objective of the Council of Europe is *"[...] to create a common democratic and legal area throughout the whole of the continent, ensuring respect for its fundamental values: human rights, democracy and the rule of law."* (Council of Europe, 2005, par. 1)

The work of the Council is to protect and promote its values for a stronger and civilized society. The fundamental values, democracy, rule of law and human rights, are indispensable to guarantee economic growth, stability and social cohesion. Its objectives are the encouragement of the European cultural diversity and identity between each other, the consolidation of democratic stability by backing reforms, and the cooperated fight against terrorism, organized crimes, human trafficking, child abuse and corruption.

4.5.2. Organization for Security and Cooperation in Europe (OSCE)

The main regional organization in Europe for security is the Organisation for Security and Co-operation in Europe (later conferred to as OSCE[36]). It is among the largest regional security organizations in

---

[35] Founding countries were the following: Belgium, Denmark, France, Ireland, Italy, Luxembourg, Netherlands, Norway, Sweden, United Kingdom.
[36] OSCE has its roots in the Conference for Security and Co-operation in Europe (CSCE), initially held in Helsinki (Finland) in 1975. The conference worked in three stages (called

the world, due to the fact that it counts 56 member countries in Europe, North America and Central Asia.

OSCE approaches cooperation for security with a multidimensional approach. This approach includes three "dimensions" or domains, identified as the following:

- first dimension, the politico-military dimension which includes a number of commitments by participating States and mechanisms for conflict prevention and resolution. The Organization also seeks to enhance military security by promoting greater openness, transparency and co-operation;
- second dimension, the economic and environmental dimension which includes the monitoring of developments in this area among participating States, with the aim of alerting them to any threat of conflict. In addition, this dimension includes the act of assisting members in the creation of economic and environmental policies and related initiatives to promote security in the OSCE region;
- third dimension, the human dimension with the aim to ensure full respect for human rights and fundamental freedoms; to abide by the rule of law; to promote the principles of democracy by building, strengthening and protecting democratic institutions; and to promote tolerance throughout the OSCE area (OSCE, (n.d.), n.p.a).

---

the "Helsinki Process"), ended in 1975. Scope of the whole process was the improvement of relations between Western European countries and Eastern European countries aligned to the Communist bloc. The crisis and fall of the Soviet Union forced a change in both scope and function of CSCE, formalized with the Charter of Paris for a New Europe (signed on 21 November 1990). This change pushed also the conference in institutionalizing itself, transforming in a fully operation international organization and thus changing its name to OSCE.

Currently, OSCE works on 18 different missions in various areas in Europe. In South-East Europe OSCE supports fields such as human rights, democratization, institution building and media development. (OSCE, 2007, p. 39-52) In Easter Europe the work focuses mainly on the countries of Ukraine, Belarus and Moldova in the fields of consolidating the rule of law, developing economic and environmental activities, build up a better relationship with the civil societies, trying for a lasting settlement of conflicts as well as fight against human trafficking. (OSCE, 2007, p. 53 - 59) In South Caucasus, the OSCE tries to support Azerbaijan (Baku) and Armenia (Yerevan) in the work of economic and environmental developments and conflict resolutions as well as working as a supporting tool for democratisation taken under account to promote the implementation of OSCE principles and its commitments by constant dialogue with the Azerbaijani authorities and the Armenian government. (OSCE, 2007, p. 60-65)

The main problem OSCE faces in Western Europe is the need to support these countries to monitor elections, improve diplomacy and resolve media issues as well as gender differences. (OSCE, 2009)

4.5.3. European Union

The European Union has originally been established with the aim of ending the frequent and bloody wars between neighbouring countries, which culminated in the Second World War. In 1950, the European Coal and Steel Community united European countries economically and politically in order to secure lasting peace. The six founders were Belgium, France, Germany, Italy, Luxembourg and the Netherlands. Later in 1957, the Treaty of Rome created the European Economic Community (EEC), or 'Common Market' (EU, (n.d.), n.p.a).

The signing of the Single European Act[37] (SEA) in 1986 transformed the European common market into a single market. Pushed by the Delors Commission[38], the SEA opened the way to political integration and an economic and monetary union (EU, (n.d.), n.p.a). An important step regarding a common security policy was established with the creation of the Common Foreign and Security Policy (CFSP) as one of the three pillars of the Maastricht Treaty[39] in 1992, which furthermore established the EU (cf. EU, (n.d.), n.p.a). With the Treaty of Amsterdam into force (1999), a European Security and Defence Policy (ESDP) was introduced and thus new tasks have been included in the Treaty on European Union.

4.5.3.1. The European Common Foreign Security Policy (CFSP) and the European Security and Defence Policy (ESDP)

The European Political Cooperation (EPC) was the name for the coordination of Europe's foreign policy. It was established in 1970 in order to allow its members to discuss and coordinate their positions on foreign affairs and, where appropriate, act in concert. With the end of the Cold War, the Soviet threat was no more and transformations in international policies were necessary. Hence, in 1992, the EPC was superseded by the Common Foreign Security Policy (CFSP) with the addition of the instruments of joint actions and common positions to the Union's foreign policy. However, these innovations proved of limited

---

[37] The SEA can be considered as the first major revision of the original Treaty of Rome. It set up the goal of the creation of a single market by 31 December 1992. The SEA was signed in Luxembourg on 17 February 1986 and in The Hague on 28 February of the same year. It came into force on the 1st of July 1987.

[38] The "Delors Commission" is the period when the European Commission was presided by Jacques Delors. This period lasted three terms, from 1985 to 1994. It is considered as one of the most productive and successful periods for the European Commission, as it was capable of reverting the growing "eurosclerosis" and the disappointment towards European institutions, which was mainly due to institutional inefficiency.

[39] The Maastricht Treaty, also known as the Treaty on European Union (TEU), is a very important milestone for the development of the contemporary European Union: it gave way to the establishment of the monetary union and Euro, as well as for the extension of the Community's competencies and the introduction of the principle of subsidiarity.

importance when the EU was unable to stop the bloodshed in Croatia and Bosnia[40]. A further upgrade of the foreign and security policy came with the establishment of the European Security and Defence Policy (ESDP) (cf. Merlingen and Ostrauskaité, 2008, pp.10-11).

The ESDP frames a common defence system. It allows the EU to develop its military and civilian capacities in the domain of conflict prevention and crisis management at international level: this way, it helps in maintaining international security and peace according to the Charter of the United Nations (Daly et al., 2012).

4.5.3.2. The Political and Security Committee

The Political and Security Committee is the monitoring body of the Common Security and Defence Policy (CSDP). Its main work is to control the political and security measures during crisis management operations in Europe, monitor the European Council's decisions and contribute to further definitions of new policies. The PSC is supported by military groups, the Politico-Military group and the military committee. (EC, Official Journal L27/1, Brussels, 2001)

The Political and Security Committee is linked with the Civilian Planning and Conduct Capability that is an important body of the European Council. Its main work is to plan and conduct civilian European Security and Defence Policy. (EC, 2009)

4.5.3.3. EU Military Committee

The European Union Military Committee evolved out of the request of the European Council, to support and recommend the Political Security Committee in military matters. During the six years, after the establishment of the ESDP and the military dimension, the EU had

---

[40] Conflicts in the Balkans are generally referred to as the "Balkan Wars" or the "Yugoslav Wars", taking place from 1991 to 2001. The Yugoslav Wars followed the breakup of Yugoslavia and originated due to the great instability present among the various successor republics and their ethnic and religious minorities. (Baker, 2015).

launched six military operations and sixteen civilian missions, also having taken into account the work with the African Union in Chad, Somalia and the Republic of Congo where EU troops are positioned to support the regional forces.

All of the missions of the MC have been successful so far, but further cooperation and coordination with other international security and defence institutions is of great importance to the EU. The Military Committee sees the added value of a stable and secure Union in the hands of the military, having rapid response and armed forces crisis management capabilities. (EC, Official Journal L27/4, Brussels, 2001)

4.5.3.4. EU Military Staff

The EU Military Committee is supported by the European Union Military Staff (EUMS), which operates in the different missions and sends military capabilities to the regions, in Europe as well as Asia, Middle East and Africa. The main tasks of the EUMS are the fields of early crisis warning, strategic planning and situation assessment. (EC, Official Journal L27/7, Brussels, 2001)

4.5.3.5. European Neighbourhood Policy

Besides the European Security and Defence Policy another main force to stabilise the European Peace and Security is the European Neighbourhood Policy. European Leaders put a big focus on the enlargement of the EU, which is a driving force for peace and stability. Co-operation and partnerships with EU neighbouring countries in the east and the south are of great importance in order to secure the existing stable situation. Therefore it is important to have well-governed countries at the borders of the European Union. A huge concern is the Balkan region, but a huge development has been achieved until 2009, which leads to the greater focus of the EU on the Southern Caucasus region to tackle problems and promote the benefits of cooperation.

Furthermore, the neighbours of the Mediterranean region suffer from illegal migration and insufficient political reform, but work together with the EU for deeper partnerships on a bilateral level. The European Union supports peace-making processes in the conflicted region in Israel with the persistent problem between Arabs and Palestinians or even security issues in the Middle East or Iran are of concerns to the European continent. (COM, 2004, p. 17-28)

4.5.3.6. *European Border and Coast Guard Agency (Frontex)*

In order to protect the European single border established in 1995 on the basis of the Schengen Treaty, Member States of the European Community decided to improve international cooperation for external security. This kind of cooperation was formalized in within the framework of the Treaty of Amsterdam. From 1999, the European Council on Justice and Home Affairs worked towards the strengthening of cooperation in the domains of security, asylum and migration. The first relevant step in this direction was the creation of External Border Practitioners Common Unit – a working group composed of members of the Strategic Committee on Immigration, Frontiers and Asylum (SCIFA)[41] and heads of national border control services.

The External Border Practitioners Common Unit worked via six Ad-Hoc Centres[42], in order to better oversee national and specific-task projects. Two years later, to improve the work of the Centres, the European Council decided further improve the work on border security by establishing – on 26 October 2004 – the European Agency for the Management of Operational Cooperation at the External Borders of the

---

[41] Established in 1999, the SCIFA deals with strategic topics regarding immigration, asylum and border management. Its area of work regards politically relevant legislative proposals, non-legislative initiatives, and horizontal and transversal issues.

[42] Risk Analysis Centre (Helsinki, Finland); Centre for Land Borders (Berlin, Germany); Air Borders Centre (Rome, Italy); Western Sea Borders Centre (Madrid, Spain); Ad-hoc Training Centre for Training (Traiskirchen, Austria); Centre of Excellence (Dover, United Kingdom); Eastern Sea Borders Centre (Piraeus, Greece).

Member States of the European Union (Frontex)[43]. Frontex took its current shape with the establishment of the European Border and Coast Guard Agency, which superseded the earlier[44].

The mission of Frontex mission is to "promote, coordinate and develop European border management in line with the EU fundamental rights charter and the concept of Integrated Border Management". Among its various tasks, there are: monitoring migratory flows and carrying out risk analysis regarding all aspects of integrated border management; the deployment of European Border and Coast Guard teams; providing support at hotspot areas with screening, debriefing, identification and fingerprinting; establishing a procedure for referring and providing initial information people who need, or wish to apply for, international protection; cooperating with the European Asylum Support Office (EASO) and national authorities.[45]

The role of Frontex and its main missions grew in importance with the growing challenge of immigrant and refugee waves from Northern Africa and Middle East, especially during the Syrian crisis, and with the menace of terrorism.

4.5.4. EUROPOL

The European Law Enforcement Cooperation works under the European Council of Ministers for Justice and Home Affairs and gets support from all member states. The main task of EUROPOL is the prevention of drug trafficking, organised crime and terrorism with a focus on criminal organisations.

The Europol mission statement is stated as the following:

---

[43] Council Regulation (EC) 2007/2004.
[44] Regulation (EU) 2016/1624.
[45] As found on http://frontex.europa.eu/about-frontex/mission-and-tasks/

"Europol will be a world-class centre of excellence to support the EU member states' fight against all forms of serious international crime and terrorism." (EUROPOL, 2009, par.2)

Europol became a full-fledged partner in 1999, evolving out of the idea of having an organization of police forces to work transnational together to tackle organised crime. Europol focuses also on terrorism, child abuse, trafficking and forgery of money.

The 10th year anniversary publication of the work of Europol says that due to the Schengen Agreements it was easy for criminal actions on a transnational level, but made it more difficult for the national police forces to tackle trafficking and organised crimes, if there would not have been any kind of cooperation between the member states. In 2000 Europol implemented the Information System (IS) with a common database. Europol was entitled to talk and cooperate with neighbouring countries too, to be able to bring best results by solving organised crime organisations.

In the recent years, the work of Europol has been re-established and set new strategic goals. Europol should supply States with operational analysis and strategic analysis due to broader analytical capabilities and should be the first platform for States to exchange information. It also has to assist countries to improve the seriousness and effectiveness of its work to prevent and combat terrorism and crimes.

Since 01 January 2010, Europol is fully transformed into an EU body. Becoming a fully included member to the European Union brings many new opportunities to work together with agencies as well as already established institutions even closer than they have already done; furthermore, the work of Europol is facilitated with third parties and the establishment of new IT-systems and the access to information which is important to counterfeit not only organised crime groups but also individual criminals in the upcoming years. (Europol, The Hague, 2009)

4.6. THE POST COLD WAR INTERNATIONAL ORDER

In the Cold War era, security between the Soviet and American bloc was kept via a risky balance system of nuclear and mass destruction weapons.

The sovereignty of other states was vicariously "loaned" to one of the superpowers in exchange for protection from possible aggression from the other. The end of the Cold War has drastically altered the global landscape and the realities of peace and security. During the Cold War the international security system was defined by the potential for dangerous nuclear confrontation between two hostile, ideologically driven systems. As the world became highly interdependent economically, a drastic shift in international relations was taking place: from a power-oriented mode of policy to economic and political methods of international law enforcement (Kistersky, 1996, p.1).

The end of the Cold War in 1989 eventually created a completely different international security environment that implicates European security changes in three major directions: (1) The European Union, NATO and OSCE tried to solidify and reinforce their institutional foundations to prepare them for new challenges. (2) The second direction of change was to reinforce existing security arrangements and enhance their resilience through a more multi-functional and multi-purpose security approach. (3) Third, NATO, the EU and the OSCE have all expanded their membership and – in the case of NATO and the EU - also their cooperation with a wide range of non-members in Western Europe, Eastern Europe, on the territory of the former Soviet Union, and even beyond (Maull, 2005, pp. 7-8).

4.7. THE CONTEMPORARY INTERNATIONAL ORDER

The contemporary international community has developed into a global one where geographical borders no longer play an important role. Moreover, contemporary international relations are now characterized by their heterogeneity. This can be seen in the existence of states with different socio-economic systems and at varying levels of social development. For the first time in the history of the human race and international relations the contemporary international community is faced with the question of survival as a consequence of the development of weapons technology as well as the neglect of the planet's ecology. These two reasons indicate the growing importance of the structural interdependence of the contemporary world and the increased difficulty involved in working on the international stage (Jazbec, (2006), p. 2).

Chapter 5

SIMILARITIES AND DIFFERENCES IN AFRICA AND EUROPE

Having analysed the development of cooperative peace and security structures on both continents, the following chapter will present similarities and differences in both continents bearing in mind the theory of common historic experiences as a precondition for the creation of a comprehensive security framework.

5.1. CONCEPT OF SOVEREIGNTY AND THE STATE SYSTEM

In order to be legitimate, a sovereign state must demonstrate responsibility by providing the basic needs of his people or at worst it can ask for international assistance. If states fail to do so, masses of people are likely to suffer and even die as a result. These circumstances usually involve major reasons for state's existence- the breakdown of peace, security, and stability. Therefore, security arrangements and international institutions play an important role. (cf. Deng, 1996, pp. xi-xvii).

The main differences between Africa and Europe consist in the development and the important role of multilateral elements in Europe, as compared to Africa. In Europe, security arrangements and institutions were established in order to prevent conflicts within the European continent as well as between East and West in Europe (cf. Maull, 2005, p.1). Not only were they established to promote peace, but also to foster cooperation and assistance. This motive remains largely absent in Africa.

As Europe's security network evolved, countries voluntarily transferred part of their authority to European institutions. Many NATO members committed themselves to the system of common defence by deploying troops in other member states. Europe also tried to combine the normative principles of the modern Westphalian order (sovereignty, territorial integrity) with those of a post-modern world (human rights, control of other member states' internal affairs) (cf. Maull, 2005, pp. 8-9).

On the opposite side there is Africa, where during colonization European powers created borders and nation states, which contain a great variety of different ethical groups. The placing of border occurred irrespectively of cultural or linguistic differences. Hence, nowadays Africa is a very fragmented continent with a high number of small and diverse economies. The integration and standardization of all these different players became one of the key challenges. The rule of law is the main principle of nation state and contributor to peace and stability, too. The three-pillar system of legislative, jurisdiction and executive as well as the monopoly of force and the authority over a clear defined geographic area are key principles for any legal state. However, after independence Africa was led by postcolonial leaders, which used authoritarian structure in order to fulfil their interests and needs, not the ones of inhabitants. (cf. Olayode, 2005, pp. 3-4) What is more, the fights between the governments and their opponents additionally increased the instability, which resulted in a high degree of the migration of refugees. The civilians who were fleeing from armed conflicts eventually crossed borders for protection. Together with these streams of migration mostly comes additional conflict. As a result, international community has to take occasional military action to facilitate assistance but often fails to pay needed attention at the crisis' root. Nowadays Africa has started to take over the primary responsibility for itself by sharing sovereignty with the establishment of regional institutions (e.g., ECOWAS) and the AU, although the international community is prepared to assist in the installation and implementation of effective state institutions. (cf. Deng, 1996)

5.2. SECURITY ARCHITECTURE

In Europe, security arrangements are a complex web of mutually reinforcing institutions, which consists of informal to highly integrated, formalized and legally binding institutions and is designated by a high degree of commonality and specificity of principles, norms, and rules (Maull, 2005, pp. 17-18). By comparison, the African security structure is rather based on regional arrangements. However, with the creation of the African Union a first step towards African security architecture has been done, that deals with conflict resolution, peace and security on the continent as a whole. (cf. Golaszinski, 2004, pp. 11-12) Unfortunately, the AU at the present is too weak. It is a meeting place only and has no supranational authority above its member states. Furthermore, there is no power equilibrium within the member states. Policies are mainly decided by the politically and economically most powerful countries.

5.3. SECURITY COMMUNITY

The disaster of the First and Second World War showed the people in Europe the necessity of peace and cooperation. After WWII in order to avoid from another intra-European war European security community has been established. Western European and North Atlantic communications were intensified and a Euro-Atlantic security community was established based on pre-existing foundations. The internalized norms and values of the community made the outbreak of a "Third World War" and henceforth nuclear destruction in Western Europe or within the NATO not imaginable. The wave of demilitarization after the end of the Cold War was therefore another crucial step towards a more secure Europe. The major institutions of this security community have been the European Communities (e.g., EU, OSCE) and NATO (cf. Maull, 2005, p. 16).

In Africa, the threat derives from the small firearms employed by dictatorships and rebel movements in order to gain political power. Countries from all over the world sell weapons to the African customers who use to pay with gold or diamonds (blood diamonds). It is astonishing that the industrialized countries who invest millions of dollars into Africa in order to increase peace and stability are at the same time the most important suppliers of weapons that are used to destabilize the whole continent. The easy availability of firearms furthermore increases the chances of armed resistance. All this makes the need for demilitarization one of the key points for increasing peace and security and presents at the same time one of the big differences between Europe and Africa.

Taking into account that Africa cannot come back to pre-colonial structures, colonialism has to be seen as the continents initial commonly shared experience leading to the fact that the creation of a security community, compared to that of Europe, is still in its infancy.

5.4. Values, Identity and Difficulty of Institutionalization

Identity in general has many considerations such as history, heritage, culture, religion, ethnicity, language, and consciousness. For instance, the EU consists of 23 official and additionally 60 indigenous languages. However, on the African continent it is estimated that there exist between 2000 and 3000 spoken languages. Europe has its own cultural system with its common values. The roots of European identity lie in ancient times, where principles such as human activity or good, rational understanding of humans etc. seemed to be given. In the Middle Ages, Christianity had a big influence on Europe's identity development whereas the knowledge of global responsibility of mankind (ecology) has become the new principle of modern Europe (Peterková, 2003, p. 1). During this development and centuries of bitter struggles and mutual destructions, Europe managed to institutionalize its (collective) memory. All European institutions are based on common values, which led to a successful operationalization of the idea of community (Bajrektarevic, 2008, p. 29).

Geographical and cultural proximity have been equally supportive and threatening to Europe's verticalization. Contrary, due to the larger size of the African continent and its diverse geographic landscape it was impossible for people to travel far distances. Hence, several ethical groups did not explore the surrounding area and had literally no contact to other, neighbouring cultural groups. This lack of shared values as a common ground for institutionalization have made it necessary to establish regional organizations, which do share values, before moving on to the creation of Pan-African institutions.

5.5. REGIONAL INTEGRATION

Europe today can be seen as one big domestic market. The implementation of the Schengen treaty abolished national borders across Europe as a result economic integration obviously increased. The Euro as the leading currency and the (almost) free flow of goods, services, humans and capital are the major pillars of the European Union. Meanwhile these policies boosted economic performance throughout Europe.

Regional integration in Africa is lacking behind. Numerous programs and initiatives failed on the broad scale. Although of good ideas it always lacked in putting policies to work. Political tensions and too much bureaucracy effectively hindered the success of any of the past programs and initiatives.

Chapter 6

CONCLUSION AND ANALYSIS OF HYPOTHESIS

This book scientifically analysed the research question of why Europe is multilateral and why Africa still is bilateral in its security structures.

Considering the first hypothesis, it can be clearly agreed that European and African security structures are the results of their historical experiences. In the case of Europe, these experiences and developments have started with the establishment of the Westphalian sovereign statehood and the following continuous creation and extension of collective and cooperative security structures over the centuries usually incorporating the most powerful players. The Europeans also were involved in the First and Second World War, and afterwards the Cold War with the dealing of the NATO alliance in the West and the Warsaw pact in the East. Europe realized that in order to avoid a new World War and to ensure stable development, security and stability countries have to work together within a united European continent. Furthermore, Europe had never experienced foreign forces dictating its development, similar to those itself had exercised on

Africa. As a result, Europe could institutionalize historic events and also established structures and networks aimed at dealing with issues and solving problems of common interest. Thereby, Europe could achieve a certain status of unity.

Applied to Africa, the assumption of economic and political stability as a precondition for peace and security becomes even more comprehensible as the Africa is still struggling with the colonial past. Hence, the majority of the conflicts and security problems of contemporary Africa can be traced back to the failure of post-colonial states, which were simply unable to maintain the inflicted European structures. Due to the extensive elimination of pre-colonial institutional structures, African leaders also could not resort to naturally developed alternative frameworks. Thus, African states continued existing in a system of European Westphalian sovereign statehood, which, due to the vast environmental differences between Africa and Europe, made this system in Africa neither a given requirement nor its implementation fully feasible.

The second hypothesis holds true- a stable economic and political environment has been the key to successful regional security structures in European continent. Security structures of Europe mostly consist of multilateral ties. This phenomenon became visible after the end of WWII and at the outbreak of the Cold War when the US strengthened the resilience of pro-Western European democracies by initiating its Marshall Plan to foster economic reconstruction and growth throughout Europe. A side effect of the implementation of the Marshall Plan was the creation of economic interdependence between Western European economies. Hence, the mere existence of a multilateral net of security organizations and the high interdependence among the European nations eventually made the abolishment of a war as a means of foreign policy feasible. Therefore, a war among European states is highly improbable (Maull, 2005, pp. 4-5).

If the region or continent is asymmetric, it is impossible to develop a real multilateralism. For instance, in American continent or in Indian subcontinent countries differs in their territorial areas as well as in the power they held and influence in the region. Thereby we can see organizations like NAFTA, which unify countries with similar indications (economically developed or at least rapidly emerging, politically enough stable). Contrary, both, Europe and Africa, are symmetric continents. Europe with its similarly developed and sized countries has been very successfully unified and has entered into multilateral ties, while, unfortunately, Africa, although all over continent equally still missing peace, economic development and political stability, has so far failed to enter into effective multilateral agreements incorporating all 53 member states. Instead, states with similar backgrounds cooperate in regional organizations continuously increasing interdependence and intensification of the multiple regionalization processes with the AU as the continental body coordinating this merging procedure. As a result, the third hypothesis is approved and acts as a precondition for confirmation of further hypothesis.

In comparison to Europe, it is still a rough and long way for the African countries, to unite (like the African Union) and to stop inequalities and jointly work together to develop and preserve a more stable and more secure continent. Based on these arguments the fourth as well as the fifth hypothesis are also confirmed- due to much suspicion and the lack of transparency between the different countries Africa failed to build a strong multilateralism. Primarily the African Union has to continue to work together not only within their own continent but also looking at the European way of dealing, due to its great experience and many partnerships around the globe. Africa will not be able to reach a level of common security and multilateralism if it is not able to dismiss intercultural and national disputes, getting rid of the corruption and promoting governmental transparency and focusing on a democratically leaded continent. The different needs and interests, which have been mentioned in the fifth hypothesis, have been also confirmed in the text, due to the different governmental view points and contradicting interests on where to focus first. Furthermore, the lack of a certain level of prosperity among member states hinders development of collective security, as African governments are more likely to put individual interests above common ones and thereby breaking the "one for all and all for one" concept.

Taking Europe as a benchmark regarding the integration of security structures, it is interesting to see how also Asia – similarly to Africa, under some profiles – presents relevant challenges that need to be discussed.

Asia lacks the "starting point" of having a single, pan-continental multilateral security structure. Prevailing security structures are bilateral and mostly asymmetric. They range from the clearly defined and enduring non-aggression security treaties, through less formal arrangements, up to the Ad hoc cooperation accords on specific issues. The presence of the multilateral regional settings is limited to a very few spots in the largest continent, and even then, they are rarely mandated with security issues in their declared scope of work. Another striking feature is that most of the existing bilateral structures have an Asian state on one side, and either peripheral or external protégé country on the other side, which makes them nearly per definition asymmetric. The examples are numerous: the US–Japan, the US– S. Korea, the US–Singapore, Russia–India, Australia–East Timor, Russia–North Korea, Japan –Malaysia, China–Pakistan, the US–Pakistan, China–Cambodia, the US–Saudi Arabia, Russia –Iran, China–Burma, India–Maldives, Iran–Syria, N. Korea–Pakistan, etc.

Indeed, Asia today resonates a mixed echo of the European past. It combines features of the pre-Napoleonic, post-Napoleonic and the League-of-Nations Europe.

By far, the largest Asian participation is with the Asia-Pacific Economic Cooperation – APEC, an organization engulfing both sides of the Pacific Rim. Nevertheless, this is a forum for member economies not of sovereign nations, a sort of a prep-com or waiting room for the World Trade Organization – WTO. Two other crosscutting settings, the

Organization of Islamic Cooperation – OIC and Non-Aligned Movement – NAM, the first with and the second without a permanent secretariat, represent the well-established political multilateral bodies. However, they are inadequate forums as neither of the two is strictly mandated with security issues. Although both trans-continental entities do have large memberships being the 2nd and 3rd largest multilateral systems, right after the UN, neither covers the entire Asian political landscape – having important Asian countries outside the system or opposing it.

Further on, one should mention the Korean Peninsula Energy Development Organization – KEDO (Nuclear) and the Iran-related Contact (Quartet/P-5 + 1) Group. In both cases, the issues dealt with are indeed security related, but they are more an asymmetric approach to deter and contain a single country by the larger front of peripheral states that are opposing a particular security policy, in this case, of North Korea and of Iran. Same was with the short-lived SEATO Pact – a defence treaty organization for SEA which was essentially dissolved as soon as the imminent threat from communism was slowed down and successfully contained within the French Indochina.

If some of the settings are reminiscent of the pre-Napoleonic Europe, the Shanghai Cooperation Organization – SCO and Cooperation Council for the Arab states of the Gulf – GCC remind us of the post-Napoleonic Europe and its Alliance of the Eastern Conservative courts (of Metternich). Both arrangements were created on a pretext of a common external ideological and geopolitical threat, on a shared status quo security consideration. Asymmetric GCC was an externally induced setting by which an American key Middle East ally Saudi Arabia gathered the grouping of the Arabian Peninsula monarchies. It has served a dual purpose; originally, to contain the leftist Nasseristic pan-Arabism which was introducing a republican type of egalitarian government in the Middle Eastern theater. It was also – after the 1979 revolution – an instrument to counter-balance the Iranian influence in the Gulf and wider Middle East. The response to the spring

2011-13 turmoil in the Middle East, including the deployment of the Saudi troops in Bahrain, and including the analysis of the role of influential Qatar-based and GCC-backed Al Jazeera TV network is the best proof of the very nature of the GCC mandate.

The SCO is internally induced and more symmetric setting. Essentially, it came into existence through a strategic Sino-Russian rapprochement[46], based, for the first time in modern history, on parity, to deter external aspirants (the US, Japan, Korea, India, Turkey and Saudi Arabia) and to keep the resources, territory, present socio-economic cultural and political regime in the Central Asia, Tibet heights and the Xinjiang Uighur province in line.

The next to consider is the Indian sub-continent's grouping, the South Asian Association for Regional Cooperation – SAARC. This organization has a well-established mandate, well staffed and versed

---

[46] Analyzing the Sino-Soviet and post-Soviet-Sino relations tempts me to compare it with the Antic Roman Empire. The monolithic block has entered its fragmentation on a seemingly rhetoric, clerical question – who would give the exclusive interpretation of the holy text: Rome or Constantinople. Clearly, the one who holds the monopoly on the interpretation has the ideological grip, which can easily be translated into a strategic advantage. It was Moscow insisting that the Soviet type of communism was the only true and authentic communism. A great schism put to an end the lasting theological but also geopolitical conflict in the antique Roman theatre. The Sino-Soviet schism culminated with the ideological and geopolitical emancipation of China, especially after the Nixon recognition of Beijing China. Besides the ideological cleavages, the socio-economic and political model of the Roman Empire was heavily contested from the 3rd century onwards. The Western Roman Empire rigidly persisted to any structural change, unable to adapt. It eroded and soon thereafter vanished from the political map. The Eastern Empire successfully reformed and Byzantium endured as a viable socio-economic and political model for another 1,000 years. Feeling the need for an urgent reshape of the declining communist system, both leaders Gorbachev and Deng Xiaoping contemplated reforms. Gorbachev eventually fractured the Soviet Union with *glasnost* and *perestroika*. Deng managed China successfully. Brave, accurate and important argumentation comes from diplomat and prolific author Kishore Mahbubani (The New Asian Hemisphere, 2008, page 44-45). Mahbubani claims that Gorbachev handed over the Soviet empire and got nothing in return, while Deng understood "the real success of Western strength and power ... China did not allow the students protesting in Tiananmen Square". Consequently, Deng drew a sharp and decisive line to avoid the fate of Russia, and allowed only *perestroika*. China has survived, even scoring the unprecedented prosperity in only the last two decades. Russia has suffered a steep decline in the aftermath of the loss of its historic empire, including the high suicide and crime rates as well as the severe alcohol problems. Gorbachev himself moved to the US, and one vodka brand labels his name.

Secretariat. However, the Organization is strikingly reminiscent of the League of Nations. The League is remembered as an altruistic setup which repeatedly failed to adequately respond to the security quests of its members as well as to the challenges and pressures of parties that were kept out of the system (e.g., Russia until well into the 1930s and the US remaining completely outside the system, and in the case of the SAARC surrounding; China, Saudi Arabia and the US). The SAARC is practically a hostage of mega confrontation of its two largest members, both confirmed nuclear powers; India and Pakistan. These two challenge each other geopolitically and ideologically. Existence of one is a negation of the existence of the other; the religiously determined nationhood of Pakistan is a negation of multiethnic India and vice verse. Additionally, the SAARC although internally induced is an asymmetric organization. It is not only the size of India, but also its position: centrality of that country makes SAARC practically impossible to operate in any field without the direct consent of India, be it commerce, communication, politics or security.

For a serious advancement of multilateralism, mutual trust, a will to compromise and achieve a common denominator through active co-existence is the key. It is hard to build a common course of action around the disproportionately big and centrally positioned member which would escape the interpretation as containment by the big or assertiveness of its center by the smaller, peripheral members.

Finally, there is the ASEAN – a grouping of 10 Southeast Asian nations[47], exercising the balanced multi-vector policy, based on the non-interference principle, internally and externally. This Jakarta/Indonesia headquartered[48] organization has a dynamic past and an ambitious current charter. It is an internally induced and relatively symmetric arrangement with the strongest members placed around its

---

[47] The membership might be extended in the future to East Timor and Papua New Guinea.
[48] Symbolic or not, the ASEAN HQ is located less than 80 miles away from the place of the historical, the NAM–precursor, the Asian–African Conference of Bandung 1955.

geographic center, like in case of the EU equilibrium with Germany-France/Britain-Italy/Poland-Spain geographically balancing each other. Situated on the geographic axis of the southern flank of the Asian landmass, the so-called growth triangle of Thailand-Malaysia-Indonesia represents the core of the ASEAN not only in economic and communication terms but also by its political leverage. The EU-like ASEAN Community Road Map (for 2015) will absorb most of the Organization's energy[49]. However, the ASEAN has managed to open its forums for the 3 + 3 group/s, and could be seen in the long run as a cumulus setting towards the wider pan-Asian forum in future.

Before closing this brief overview, let us mention two recently inaugurated informal forums, both based on the external calls for a burden sharing. One, with a jingoistic-coined name by the Wall Street bankers[50] - BRI(I)C/S, so far includes two important Asian economic, demographic and political powerhouses (India and China), and one peripheral (Russia). Indonesia, Turkey, Saudi Arabia, Pakistan, Kazakhstan, Iran are a few additional Asian countries whose national pride and pragmatic interests are advocating a BRIC membership. The G–20, the other informal forum, is also assembled on the Ad hoc (pro bono) basis following the need of the G–7 to achieve a larger approval and support for its monetary (currency exchange accord) and financial (austerity) actions introduced in the aftermath of still unsettled financial crisis. Nevertheless, the BRIC and G-20 have not provided the Asian

---

[49] Comparisons pose an inaccuracy risks as history often finds a way to repeat itself, but optimism finally prevails. Tentatively, we can situate the ASEAN today, where the pre-Maastricht EU was between the Merge Treaty and the Single European Act.

[50] The acronym was originally coined by Jim O'Neill, a chief global economist of Goldman Sachs, in his 2001 document report: "Building Better Global Economic BRICs". This document was elaborating on countries which may provide the West with the socially, economically and politically cheap primary commodities and undemanding labor force, finally suggesting to the West to balance such trade by exporting its high-prized final products in return. The paper did not foresee either creation of any BRIC grouping or the nomadic change of venue places of its periodic meetings. O'Neill initially tipped Brazil, Russia, India and China, although at recent meetings South Africa was invited (BRICS) with the pending Indonesia (BRIICS).

participating states either with the more leverage in the Bretton Woods institutions besides a burden sharing, or have they helped to tackle the indigenous Asian security problems. Appealing for the national pride, however, both informal gatherings may divert the necessary resources and attention to Asian states from their pressing domestic, pan-continental issues.

Yet, besides the UN system machinery of the Geneva-based Disarmament committee, the UN Security Council, the Organization for the Prohibition of Chemical Weapons – OPCW and International Atomic Energy Agency – IAEA (or CTBTO), even the ASEAN Asians (as the most multilateralized Asians) have no suitable standing forum to tackle and solve their security issues. An organization similar to the Council of Europe or the OSCE is still far from emerging on Asian soil.

Our history warns. Nevertheless, it also provides a hope: the pre-CSCE (pre-Helsinki) Europe was indeed a dangerous place to live in. The sharp geopolitical and ideological default line was passing through the very heart of Europe, cutting it into halves. The southern Europe was practically sealed off by notorious dictatorships; in Greece (Colonel Junta), Spain (Franco) and Portugal (Salazar), with Turkey witnessing several of its governments toppled by the secular and omnipotent military establishment, with inverted Albania and a (non-Europe minded) non-allied, Tito's Yugoslavia. Two powerful instruments of the US military presence (NATO) and of the Soviets (Warsaw pact) in Europe were keeping huge standing armies, enormous stockpiles of conventional as well as the ABC weaponry and delivery systems, practically next to each other. By far and large, European borders were not mutually recognized. Essentially, the west rejected to even recognize many of the Eastern European, Soviet dominated/installed governments.

FUTURE OUTLOOK

With the implementation of the ESDP the EU wants to maintain the security of the European continent primarily by its own resources and some NATO assistance. As the ESDP bases on the voluntary commitment of the member states of the EU, one of the main barriers in terms of its development is the national sovereignty of each single state. Therefore the future of the ESDP will depend for the most part on the political will of the member states and European military capacities. For the European security policy it will be vital that all the member states collectively commit themselves to common security interests and practices in order to develop a common European strategic culture and to be taken serious internationally (Alt, 2006, pp.13-14). By contrast to Europe's continuously increasing political and security merging, African efforts at building regional peace and security mechanisms will remain improbable, or at best unsustainable, if the continent is unable to secure process on economic development and democratic consolidation. Africa's excessive external economic dependence, and its resulting sensibility to fluctuations in the international financial systems, leads to the conclusion that its perpetual economic difficulties considerably limit the continent's potential and capacity to lead itself towards unity and the creation of sustainable regional peace and security structures.

Nonetheless, the progress towards building such structures in form of regional peacekeeping and conflict management, which attempt addressing the full range of security factors, (as exercised by ECOWAS, IGAD, etc.) has already started and appears irreversible. (cf. Francis, 2006, pp. 241-243) Additionally, growing international interest in the continent caused by its vast natural resources provides a unique opportunity to eventually also gain economic independency.

Given these developments and conditions the 21st century could truly become the "African Century".

AFTERWORD

Throughout the most of human evolution, progress and its horizontal transmission was an extremely slow, occasional and tedious process. Well into the classic period of Alexander the Macedonian and his glorious Alexandrian library, the speed of our knowledge transfers – however moderate, analogue and conservative – was still always surpassing snail-like cycles of our breakthroughs. When our sporadic breakthroughs finally turned to be faster than the velocity of their infrequent transmissions – that very event marked the point of our departure.

Simply, our civilizations started to significantly differentiate from each other in their respective techno-agrarian, politico-military, ethno-religious and ideological, and economic setups. In the eve of grand discoveries, that very event transformed wars and famine from the low-impact and local, into the bigger and cross-continental. Faster cycles of technological breakthroughs, patents and discoveries than their own transfers, primarily occurred on the Old continent.

That occurrence, with all its reorganizational effects, radically reconfigured societies to the point of polarizing world onto the two: colonizers and colonized.

For the past few centuries, Africa lived fear but dreamt a hope of Europeans – all for the sake of modern times. From WWI to www, is this modernity of internet age, with all the suddenly reviled breakthroughs and their instant transmission, now harboring us in a bay of fairness, harmony and overall reconciliation?

Shall we stop short at the Kantian dream, or continue to the Hobbesian realities and grasp for an objective, geopolitical definition of currents?

This book is our modest contribution to the most pressing of all debates: our common Afro-European futures. We are happy if You saw it that way too.

Anis Bajrektarevic and Giuliano Luongo
The Authors

REFERENCES

Books and Articles

Adi, H., Devereux, D., Locatelli, F., and Oduor Ndege, G (2005). *Encyclopedia of African History. Volume 1: A-G.* New York: Fitzroy Dearborn.

Adu Boahen, A. (1900). *General History of Africa. VII African under Colonial Domination 1880-1935.* Paris: United Nations Educational, Scientific and Cultural Organization.

Ahmida, A. (1994). *The Making of Modern Libya. State Formation, Colonization and Resistance, 1830-1932.* Albany: State University of New York.

Alt, J. (2006). *The Future of the European Security and Defence Policy.* Maxwell Air Force Base: Air Command and Staff College, Air University.

Asch R. G. (1997). The Thirty Years War: The Holy Roman Empire and Europe, 1618-1648. New York: Palgrave.

Bajrektarevic A. H. (2008). *Institutionalization of Historical Experiences: Europe and Asia: Same Quest, Different Results, Common Futures.*

Baker, C. (2015). *The Yugoslav Wars of the 1990s*. New York: Palgrave.

Birmingham D. (2003). *The Decolonization of Africa*. London: University College London.

Boemeke M., Feldman G., and Glaser E. (1998). *The Treaty of Versailles – A Reassessment after 75 years*. Cambridge: Cambridge University Press.

Buzan B., and Waever O. (2003). *Regions and Powers: The Structure of International Security*. Cambridge: Cambridge University Press.

Calchi Novati G., and Valsecchi, P. (2005). *Africa: la storia ritrovata. Dalle prime forme politiche agli stati nazionali.* [*Africa: the retrieved history. From the early political forms to national States*] Rome: Carocci.

Cameron, R., and Neal, L. (2003). *A concise Economic History of the World – 4th edition*. New York: Oxford University Press.

Chabal P., and Vidal N. (2008). *Angola: The Weight of History*. New York: Columbia University Press.

Daly, P., Michael Feener, R., and Reid, A. (2012). *From the Ground Up: Perspectives on Post-Tsunami and Post-Conflict Aceh*. Singapore: ISEAS.

De Pradt, M. (1816). *The Congress of Vienna*. London: J. Moyes.

De Lutiis, G. (1996). *Il lato oscuro del potere. Associazioni politiche e strutture paramilitari segrete dal 1946 a oggi.* [*The dark side of power. Political associations and secret paramilitary structures from 1946 to present day*] Rome: Editori Riuniti.

Deng, F. M. (1996). *Sovereignty as Responsibility: Conflict Management in Africa*. Washington D.C.: The Brookings Institution.

DeRouen K., Jr. (2005). *Defence and Security – A Compendium of National Forces and Securities Policies*. Santa Barbara: ABC-CLIO, Inc.

DFID Report (2001). The Causes of Conflict in Africa. London: Cabinet Sub-Committee on Conflict Prevention in Africa.

Djamson, E. (1976). *The Dynamics of Euro-African Co-operation*. The Hague: Martinus Nijhoff.

Duignan, P. (2000). *NATO: Its Past, Present, and Future*. Stanford: Stanford University.

Elias, T. O. (1988). *Africa and the Development of International Law*. Dordrecht: Kluwer Academic Publishers.

European Commission (22 January 2001). Official Journal L 27. Council Decision on setting up the European Military Committee. Brussels

European Commission (22 January 2001). Official Journal L27/4. Council Decision on setting up the Political and Security Committee. Brussels

European Police Office (2009). Ten years of Europol 1999-2009. The Hague.

Europol (2009), Ten years of Europol 1999 – 2009, Anniversary Publication, Corporate Communication. The Hague.

Extractive Industry Transparency Initiative. (2009). EITI Fact Sheet. Oslo: EITI International Secretariat.

Ferdowski, M. A. (2004). *Afrika – ein verlorener Kontinent? [Africa – a lost continent?]* Munich: Wilhelm Fink Verlag.

Francis D. (2006). *Uniting Africa: Building regional peace and security structures*. Adlershot: Ashgate Publishing Limited.

Gann, L., and Duignan, P. (1977). *The Rulers of German Africa. 1884-1914*. Stanford: Stanford University Press.

Gentili, A. (1995). *Il Leone e il Cacciatore: Storia dell'Africa Sub-Sahariana*. [*The lion and the hunter: History of Sub-Saharan Africa*] Rome: Carocci.

Gross, L. (1984). *Essays on International Law and Organization*. New York: Transnational Publisher, Inc.

Herbst, J. (2000). *States and power in Africa: comparative lessons in authority and control*. Princeton: Princeton Universtiy Press.

Johnson, D. (1976). *The Cambridge History of Africa. c.17900-c.1870 (Volume 5)*. Cambridge: Cambridge University Press.

Jewsiewicki, B. (1986). *The Cambridge History of Africa. c.1905-c.1940 (Volume 7)*. Cambridge: Cambridge University Press.

Khapoya, V. (1998). *The African Experience: An Introduction*. Prentice Hall.

Kreijen G. (2004). *State Failure, Sovereignty and Effectiveness*. Leiden: Brill Academic Publishers.

MacKenzie, J.M. (1983). *The partition of Africa*. New York: Methuen & Co.

Mastny V., and Byrne M. (2005). *A cardboard castle? - An inside history of the Warsaw Pact, 1955-1991*. Budapest: Central European University Press.

Mehler, A., and Besdedau, M. (2005). *Resource Politics in Sub-Saharan Africa*. Hamburg: Hamburg African Studies.

Merlingen M., and Ostrauskaité R. (2008). *European Security and Defence Policy: An Implementation Perspective*. New York: Routledge.

Morell, J. (1854). *Algeria. The Topography and History, Political, Social, and Natural, of French Africa*. London: Nathaniel Cooke, Milford House, Strand.

Murison K. (2004). *Africa South of the Sahara, 33rd edition*. London: The Gresham Press.

Nugent, P. (2004). *Africa: Since Independence*. New York: Palgrave McMillan.

Organization of African Unity (1963). Charter of the Organization of African Unity. Addis Ababa.

OSCE (2007). OSCE Handbook, OSCE Press and Public Information Section, Vienna

OSCE (2008). OSCE Handbook of 2008. Vienna.

OSCE (2009), Annual Report 2008, Office of the Secretary General, Edited by Sharman Esarey, Vienna.

OSCE (n.d.). The three OSCE dimensions. http://www.osce.org/item/18807.html. Access: November 22, 2009.

References

Oyebade A., and Alao A. (1998). *Africa after the Cold War: The changing perspectives on security*. Asmara: Africa World Press Inc.

Perras, A. (2004). *Carl Peters and German Imperialism: 1856-1918. A Political Biography*. New York: Oxford University Press

Pilbeam, P. (1995). *Themes in modern European History. 1780-1830*. New York: Routledge.

Rustad, S., Le Billon, P., Lujala, P. (2017). « Has the Extractive Industries Transparency Initiative been a success? Identifying and evaluating EITI goals". *Resource Policy*, 51:151-162.

Sanderson, G.N. (1985). *The Cambridge History of Africa. c.1870-c.1905 (Volume 6)*. Cambridge: Cambridge University Press.

Sheehan M. (1996). *Balance of Power – History and Theory*. London: Routledge.

Shillington, K. (2005). *History of Africa*. Palgrave MacMillan.

Smith M. A., and Timmins G. (2001). *Uncertain Europe: Building a New European Security Order?*. London: Routledge.

United Nations Economic Commission for Africa. (2008). Securing our Future. Report of the Commission on HIV/AIDS and Governance in Africa.

United Nations. (2009). Millennium Development Goals Report 2009. New York: United Nations Department of Economic and Social Affairs.

Wayman F., Diehl P. (1994). *Reconstructing Realpolitik*. Michigan: The University of Michigan Press.

Weiss, T. G. (1993). *Collective security in a changing world*. London: Lynne Rienner Publishers, Inc.

Werbner H., Ranger T. (1996). *Postcolonial Identities in Africa*. London: Zed Books Ltd.

Zacarias A. (1999). *Security and the State in Southern Africa*. London: I. B. Tauris & Co. Limited.

Online Resources

Africa: British Colonies-history of British colonial rule in Africa, precolonial racial and ethnic relations in British colonial Africa. http://encyclopedia.jrank.org/articles/pages/5920/Africa-British-Colonies.html. Access: March 09, 2010.

African Union (n.d.). Regional Economic Communities (RECs): Economic Community of Central African States. http://www.africa-union.org/root/au/recs/eccas.htm. Access: November 11, 2009.

African Union. (2009). African Union in a Nutshell. http://www.africa-union.org/root/au/AboutAu/au_in_a_nutshell_en.htm. Access on 25 October, 2009.

Ball N., Kayode J. (n.d.). Security Sector Governance in Africa: A Handbook. http://www.ssronline.org/ssg_a/index.cfm?id=115&p=19. Accessed: November 12, 2009.

BBC (2009). BBC News Timeline: Angola. http://news.bbc.co.uk/2/hi/africa/country_profiles/1839740.stm. Accessed: November 16, 2009.

BBC (n.d.). The Story of Africa: African History from the dawn of time.... http://www.bbc.co.uk/worldservice/africa/features/storyofafrica/12chapter8.shtml. Accessed: November 10, 2009.

Britannica (n.d.). Balance of Power. http://www.britannica.com/EBchecked/topic/473296/balance-of-power. Accessed: November 13, 2009.

Britannica (n.d.). Collective Security. http://www.britannica.com/EBchecked/topic/125567/collective-security. Access: November 17, 2009.

Britannica (n.d.). War of the Austrian Succession. http://www.britannica.com/EBchecked/topic/44477/War-of-the-Austrian-Succession. Accessed: November 15, 2009.

British Colonialism. http://countrystudies.us/south-africa/11.htm. Accessed: March 09, 2010.

CDD West Africa (n.d.). Center for Democracy and Development: About Us. http://cddwestafrica.org/index.php?option=com_content&view=article&id=96:about-us&catid=25:about-cdd&Itemid=61. Accessed: November 11, 2009.

CIA Factbook (2009). Cape Verde. https://www.cia.gov/library/publications/the-world-factbook/geos/cv.html. Accessed: November 12, 2009.

CoE (n.d.). The Council of Europe in brief – Our objectives. http://www.coe.int/aboutcoe/index.asp?page=nosobjectifs&l=en. Accessed: November 22, 2009.

CoE (n.d.). The Council of Europe in brief – Who we are. http://www.coe.int/aboutcoe/index.asp. Accessed: November 22, 2009.

Commonwealth of Nations (n.d.). Who we are: The Commonwealth. http://www.thecommonwealth.org/Internal/191086/191247/the_commonwealth/. Access: November 11, 2009.

Council of Europe (2009), Our Mission. http://www.coe.int/aboutCoe/index.asp?page=nosObjectifs&l=en. Access: 7 November, 2009.

Council of Europe (2009), Parliamentary Assembly. http://assembly.coe.int/Main.asp?Link=/AboutUs/APCE_history.htm. Access on 7 November, 2009.

CPLP (n.d.). Comunidad dos Países de Língua Portuguesa. http://www.cplp.org/id-46.aspx. Access: November 17, 2009.

Deflem M. (1994). Law Enforcement in British Colonial Africa. http://www.cas.sc.edu/socy/faculty/deflem/zcolpol.html. Access: November 11, 2009.

EAC Portal (n.d.). East African Community Portal: About EAC. http://www.eac.int/about-eac.html. Access: November 13, 2009.

EASBRIG (n.d.). Eastern African Standby Brigade Coordination Mechanism. http://www.easbrig.org/about.php. Access: November 14, 2009.

ECOWAS (n.d.). Achievements of ECOWAS: Regional Peace and Security. http://www.sec.ecowas.int/sitecedeao/english/peace.htm. Access: November 13, 2009.

ECOWAS (n.d.). Achievements of ECOWS: Regional Peace and Security. http://www.sec.ecowas.int/sitecedeao/english/peace.htm. Access: November 13, 2009.

Embassy of People's Republic of China in the Republic of South Africa. (2009) China, Sierra Leone vow to further enhance friendly ties. http://www.chinese-embassy.org.za/eng/zfgx/t564444.htm Access: March 21, 2010.

Embassy of People's Republic of China in the Republic of South Africa. (2009). China pledges continued aid to Sierra Leone amid global slump. http://www.chinese-embassy.org.za/eng/zfgx/t564701.htm Access: March 21, 2010.

Embassy of People's Republic of China in the Republic of South Africa. (2009). Chinese, South African leaders agree to deepen bilateral relations. http://www.chinese-embassy.org.za/eng/zt/tenthanniversary/t605847.htm Access: March 21,2010.

Embassy of People's Republic of China in the Republic of South Africa. (2009). Zimbabwe appeals for Chinese loans to buy road equipment. http://www.chinese-embassy.org.za/eng/zfgx/t569134.htm Access: 21 March, 2010.

Embassy of People's Republic of China in the Republic of South Africa. (2009). China justifies veto of Zimbabwe sanctions. http://www.chinese-embassy.org.za/eng/zfgx/t569372.htm Access: 21 March, 2010.

Embassy of People's Republic of China in the Republic of South Africa. (2009). China pledges to work with Sudan to expand co-op in all fields. http://www.chinese-emba.ssy.org.za/eng/zfgx/t573354.htm Access: 21 March, 2010.

Embassy of People's Republic of China in the Republic of South Africa. (2009). Full text of Chinese premier's speech at 4th Ministerial Conference of Forum on China-Africa Cooperation.

http://www.chinese-embassy.org.za/eng/zfgx/t625493.htm Access: 21 March, 2010.

Europa (n.d.). 'New-look' NATO. http://europa.eu/scadplus/glossary/newlook_nato_en.htm. Access: November 22, 2009.

Europa (n.d.). Collective Defence. http://europa.eu/scadplus/glossary/collective_defence_en.htm. Access: November 22, 2009.

Europa (n.d.). Glossary: European Security and Defence Policy (ESDP). http://europa.eu/scadplus/glossary/european_security_defence_policy_en.htm. Access: November 23, 2009.

Europa (n.d.). Summaries of EU legislation: The Single European Act. http://europa.eu/legislation_summaries/institutional_affairs/treaties/treaties_singleact_en.htm. Access: November 23, 2009.

Europa (n.d.). Summaries of EU legislation: Treaty of Maastricht on European Union. http://europa.eu/legislation_summaries/economic_and_monetary_affairs/institutional_and_economic_framework/treaties_maastricht_en.htm. Access: NOV 23, 2009.

Europa (n.d.). The history of the European Union. http://europa.eu/abc/history/index_en.htm. Access: November 23, 2009.

European Commission (2004), European Neighbourhood Policy. http://ec.europa.eu/world/enp/pdf/strategy/strategy_paper_en.pdf., Brussels Access: 20 November, 2009.

European Council (2009), Civilian Planning and Conduct Capabilities, http://www.consilium.europa.eu/-showPage.aspx?id=1487&lang=EN. Access: 12 November, 2009.

Europol (2009), mission statement. http://www.europol.europa.eu/index.asp?page=facts. Access: 5 November, 2009.

Extractive Industry Transparency Initiative. (2009). Principles and Criteria. http://eitransparency.org/eiti. Access: 03 November, 2009.

Foreign and Commonwealth Office (2009). Sub Saharan Africa – Cape Verde. http://www.fco.gov.uk/en/travel-and-living-abroad/travel-advice-by-country/country-profile/sub-saharan-africa/cape-verde?profile= politics. Access: November 10, 2009.

References

Foreign Policy (2009). The Failed State Index 2009. http://www.foreignpolicy.com/articles/2009/06/22/2009_failed_states_index_interactive_map_and_rankings. Accessed: November 15. 2009.

Ganser, D (2005). Terrorism in Western Europe: An Approach to NATO's Secret Stay-Behind Armies, The Whitehead Journal of Diplomacy and International Relations, Winter/Spring 2005. Available at http://www.physics911.net/pdf/DanieleGanser_Terrorism_in_Western_Europe-1.pdf Accessed: October 19, 2016.

German Federal Ministry for Economic Cooperation and Development. (2009). Countries and Regions. http://www.bmz.de/en/countries/partnercountries/kamerun/index.html. Accessed: November 01, 2009.

Global Security Org (n.d.). Weapons of Mass Destruction (WMD). http://www.globalsecurity.org/wmd/world/rsa/nuke.htm. Accessed: November 12, 2009.

Golaszinski U. (2004). Africa's Evolving Security Structure. http://library.fes.de/pdf-files/iez/02580.pdf. Access: November 30, 2009.

Gordon, K. (2008). The Origins of Westphalian Sovereignty. http://www.wou.edu/las/socsci/history/thesis%2008/KellyGordonWestphalianSovereignty.pdf. Accessed: November 13, 2009.

Group of 77. (2009). About the Group of 77. http://www.g77.org. Accessed: 30 November, 2009.

IGAD (2007). Intergovernmental Authority on development: Peace and Security. http://www.igad.org/index.php?option=com_content&task=view&id=46&Itemid=57. Accessed: November 14, 2009.

IGAD (n.d.). http://www.igad.org/index.php?option=com_content&task=view&id=43&Itemid=53. Accessed: November 13, 2009.

ISS Africa (1999). Bilateral Treaties, Agreements and Related Issues. http://www.issafrica.org/Pubs/Monographs/No43/BilateralTreaties.html. Accessed: November 9, 2009.

References

ISS Africa (1999). Building Security in Southern Africa. http://www.issafrica.org/Pubs/Monographs/No43/BilateralTreaties.html. Accessed: November 12, 2009.

ISS Africa (n.d.). ISS Africa: About Us. http://www.issafrica.org/index.php?link_id=1&link_type=13&tmpl_id=3. Accessed: November 12, 2009.

ISS Africa (n.d.). Kenya - Security Information. http://www.issafrica.org/AF/profiles/Kenya/SecInfo.html. Accessed: November 10, 2009.

ISS Africa (n.d.). Nigeria – Fact File. http://www.issafrica.org/index.php?link_id=14&slink_id=4157&link_type=12&slink_type=12&tmpl_id=3. Accessed: November 12, 2009.

ISS Africa (n.d.). Nigeria – History and Politics. http://www.issafrica.org/AF/profiles/Nigeria/Politics.html. Accessed: November 12, 2009.

ISS Africa (n.d.). Nigeria – Security Information. http://www.issafrica.org/AF/profiles/nigeria/SecInfo.html. Accessed: November 12, 2009.

ISS Africa (n.d.). Profile: Economic Community of West African States (ECOWAS). http://www.iss.co.za/index.php?link_id=3893&slink_id=3066&link_type=12&slink_type=12&tmpl_id=3. Accessed: November 13, 2009.

ISS Africa (n.d.). Protocol on Politics, Defence and Security Cooperation. http://www.issafrica.org/AF/RegOrg/unity_to_union/pdfs/sadc/1Protocol_on_Defence_Organ.pdf. Accessed: November 12, 2009.

ISS Africa (n.d.). Sierra Leone: Fact Sheet. http://www.issafrica.org/index.php?link_id=14&slink_id=3474&link_type=12&slink_type=12&tmpl_id=3. Accessed: November 10, 2009.

Italian Ministry of Foreign Affairs. (2009). Peace Process and Security. http://www.esteri.it/MAE/EN/Politica_Estera/Aree_Geografiche/Africa/Processi_di_pacesicurezza.htm. Accessed: 01 November 2009.

Jazbec M. (2006). Diplomacy and Security after the End of the Cold War: The Change in Paradigm. http://www.da-vienna.ac.at/UserFiles/reden/JAZBEC06112006.pdf. Accessed: November 2 4, 2009.

Kistersky, L. (1996). New Dimensions of the International Security System after the Cold War. http://iis-db.stanford.edu/pubs/10277/kistersky.pdf. Accessed: November 24, 2009.

Library of Congress (2007). Country Profile, Kenya. http://lcweb2.loc.gov/frd/cs/profiles/Kenya.pdf. Accessed: November 7, 2009.

Library of Congress Country Studies (1991). Nigeria – European Slave Trade in West Africa. http://lcweb2.loc.gov/cgi-bin/query/r?frd/cstdy:@field%28DOCID+ng0019%29. Accessed: November 12, 2009.

Maull H.W. (2005). Security Cooperation in Europe and Pacific Asia: A Comparative Analysis. http://www.politik.uni-trier.de/mitarbeiter/maull/pubs/securitycoop.pdf. Accessed: November 24, 2009.

Moodie M. (2000). Cooperative Security: Implications for National Security and International Relations. http://www.cmc.sandia.gov/cmc-papers/sand98-050514.pdf. Accessed: November 30, 2009.

Olayode K. (2005). Reinventing the African State: Issues and Challenges for Building a developmental State. http://www.codesria.org/Links/conferences/general_assembly11/papers/olayode.pdf. Accessed: November 29, 2009.

Organisation Internationale de la Francophonie. (2009). Qui sommes nous? http://www.francophonie.org. Accessed: 31 November, 2009.

Organisation of Islamic Conference. (2009). About OIC http://www.oic-oci.org. Access: 25 November, 2009.

OSCE (2009), Field operations. http://www.conect.at/uploads/tx_posseminar/OSCE_Ruehrig_VoIP.pdf Accessed: November 11, 2009.

OSCE (2009), Field operations. http://www.osce.org/about/13510.html. Accessed: 11 November, 2009.

Paulsen T. (1996). Machiavelli und die Idee der Staatsräson. http://www.staatswissenschaft.de/pdf/IFSNachrichten2.pdf. Accessed: November 13, 2009.

Peterková J. (2003). The Role of Cultural Heritage in the Process of Mutual Communication and Creation of Consciousness of Common Cultural Identity. http://www.kakanien.ac.at/beitr/fallstudie/JPeterkova1.pdf. Accessed: November 30, 2009.

PRLog Free Press Release (2008). Defence & Security Report South Africa. http://www.prlog.org/10072672-defence-security-report-south-africa.html. Accessed: November 9, 2009.

Purefoy Ch. (2009). Nigeria hopes peace can bring big China deals. http://www.cnn.com/2009/WORLD/africa/10/21/nigeria.oil.deal/index.html. Accessed: November 12, 2009.

Republic of Kenya – Ministry of Foreign Affairs (2007). Foreign Policy.http://www.mfa.go.ke/mfacms/index.php?option=com_content&task=view&id=13&Itemid=31&limit=1&limitstart=1. Accessed: November 8, 2009.

Schekulin M. (2007). Trade History and Organization (WS 2007) – Handout. Lecture Slides from the Course in Trade History and Organizations, IMC Krems.

Schimmer, R. (2009). Belgian Congo. 6 paragraphs. http://www.yale.edu/gsp/colonial/belgian_congo/index.html. Accessed: November 30, 2009.

Shah A. (2004). Nigeria and Oil. http://www.globalissues.org/article/86/nigeria-and-oil. Accessed: November 12, 2009.

The World Bank (2009). Cape Verde – Country Brief. http://web.worldbank.org/WBSITE/EXTERNAL/COUNTRIES/AFRICAEXT/CAPEVERDEEXTN/0,,menuPK:349633~pagePK:141132~piPK:141107~theSitePK:349623,00.html. Accessed: November 9, 2009.

UN (2009). UNAMSIL: United Nations Mission to Sierra Leone. http://www.un.org/Depts/dpko/missions/unamsil/index.html. Accessed: November 20, 2009.

UN (n.d.). About the United Nations/History. http://www.un.org/aboutun/history.htm. Accessed: November 20, 2009.

UN (n.d.). Charter of the United Nations – Chapter 1: Purposes and Principles. http://www.un.org/en/documents/charter/chapter1.shtml. Accessed: November 21, 2009.

UN (n.d.). UN at a Glance – Overview. http://www.un.org/en/aboutun/index.shtml. Accessed: November 21, 2009.

UN (n.d.). United Nations Peacebuilding Missions. http://www.un.org/peace/peacebuilding/. Access: November 21, 2009.

UNDP (n.d.). A World of Development experience. http://www.undp.org/about/. Accessed: November 18, 2009.

UNDP (n.d.). About the MDGs: Basics. http://www.undp.org/mdg/basics.shtml. Accessed: November 12, 2009.

UNDP (n.d.). UNDP in Africa. http://www.undp.org/africa/#. Access: November 18, 2009.

United Nations Economic Commission for Africa. (2009). About ECA. http://www.uneca.org. Accessed: 29 October, 2009.

United Nations. (2009). http://www.un.org. Accessed: 25. November, 2009.

United Nations. (2009). Millenium Development Goals. http://www.un.org/millenniumgoals/bkgd.shtml. Accessed: November 02, 2009.

US Department of State (2009). Background Note: Cape Verde. http://www.state.gov/r/pa/ei/bgn/2835.htm. Accessed: November 10, 2009.

USHMM (n.d.). Treaty of Versailles, 1919. http://www.ushmm.org/wlc/article.php?lang=en&ModuleId=10005425. Accessed: November 17, 2009.

AUTHOR PROFILES

Anis H. Bajrektarević, professor and chairperson for international law and global political studies, teaches at the Swiss University of Genève. Besides this very title, he authored the books: *FB – Geopolitics of Technology* (Addleton, New York 2013); *Geopolitics* (DB, 2014), *Geopolitics – Energy – Technology* (Nova, 2015); *Cybersecurity & Nuclear Commerce* (LAP, Germany 2016). He is both a teaching and research professor on subjects such as the Geopolitics; International and EU Law; Sustainable Development (institutions and instruments). On the subject Geopolitical Affairs alone, the Professor has over 1,200 teaching hours at his main Austrian and Swiss universities as well as in many countries on all meridians. As prolific writer and frequent contributor, his writings are published in over 50 countries in all five continents, and translated in 20 languages worldwide.

Giuliano Luongo is the Director of the African Studies Research Programme at IsAG – Institute for Advanced Studies in Geopolitics, Rome. He has worked from 2009 in international cooperation. His areas of expertise range from international politics to economic and social development. He is the author of various articles and essays in international politics and economics, published and translated in different countries.

INDEX

A

AFRC (Armed Forces Revolutionary Council), xxi
AIDS (Acquired Immunodeficiency Syndrome), xxi, 53, 66, 117
ALDE (Alliance of Liberals and Democrats for Europe), xxi
AMISOM (African Union Mission in Somalia), xxi, 42
ASSN (African Security Sector Network), xxi
AU (African Union), xxi, 36, 37, 38, 39, 42, 43, 44, 50, 52, 61, 63, 87, 95, 101, 118

B

Berlin Conference, 7, 9, 13, 14, 17, 18, 19, 23, 65

C

CDD (Center for Development and Democracy), xxi, 48, 119
CDS (Defence and Security Commission), xxi, 39
CEWARN (Early Warning and Early Response Mechanism), xxi, 37
CoE (Council of Europe), xxi, 82, 107, 119
Collective Defence, 76, 121
Congress of Vienna, 71, 114
COPAX (Council for Peace and Security in Central Africa), xxi, 38
CPCC (Civilian Planning and Conduct Capabilities), xxi, 121

E

EASBRIG (Eastern African Standby Brigade), xxi, 35, 37, 119
ECCAS (Economic Community of Central African States), xxi, 34, 38, 118
ECOMOG (Economic Community of West African States Monitoring Group), xxi, 35, 36
ECOWAS (Economic Community of West African States), xxi, 34, 35, 36, 64, 95, 110, 120, 123

Index

EDG (European Democrat Group), xxi
EEC (European Economic Community), xxi, 84
EITI (Extractive Industries Transparency Initiative), xxi, 45, 46, 47, 115, 117
EPC (European Political Cooperation), xxii, 85
EPP (European People's Party), xxii
ESDP (European Security and Defence Policy), xxii, 85, 86, 87, 109, 113, 116, 121
EU (European Union), x, xvi, xxii, xxiii, 40, 46, 61, 63, 64, 65, 66, 76, 84, 85, 86, 87, 88, 89, 90, 91, 96, 97, 98, 106, 109, 121
EUMC (European Union Military Committee), xxii, 86
EUMS (European Union Military Staff), xxii, 87

F

FLS (Front Line States), xxii
FOMAC (Central African Multinational Force), xxii, 39

G

GATT (General Agreement on Tariffs and Trade), xxii, 76

H

HIV (Human Immunodeficiency Virus), xxii, 31, 53, 62, 66, 117
HoSG (Heads of State and Government), xxii, 38

I

IBRD (International Bank for Reconstruction and Development), xxii, 75
ICPAT (IGAD Capacity Building Programme Against Terrorism), xxii, 37
IGAD (Inter-Governmental Authority on Development), xxii, 34, 36, 37, 110, 122
IMF (International Monetary Fund), xxii, 63, 75
ISDSC (Inter-State Defence and Security Co-operation), xxii, 38
ISPDC (Interstate, Politics and Diplomacy Committee), xxii, 38
ISS (Institute for Security Studies), xxii, 15, 28, 35, 38, 48, 63, 122, 123
ITO (International Trade Organization), xxii, 75

M

MARAC (Central African Multinational Force), xxii, 39
MCO (Ministerial Committee of the Organ), xxii, 38
MCPMR (Mechanism for Conflict Prevention, Management and Resolution), xxii, 42
MDGs (Millennium Development Goals), xxii, 29, 53, 117, 126

N

NATO (North Atlantic Treaty Organization), xxii, 40, 76, 77, 78, 91, 94, 96, 99, 107, 109, 115, 121, 122
NEPAD (New Partnership for Africa's Development), xxii, 49

NGO (Non Governmental Organization), xxii
NSDAP (Nationalsozialistische Deutsche Arbeiterpartei), xxii, 73

O

OAU (Organization of African Unity), xxii, 40, 41, 42, 49, 116
OIC (Organization for Islamic Conference), xxii, 44, 45, 103, 124
OPDSC (SADC Organ on Politics, Defence and Security Cooperation), xxiii, 38
OSCE (Organization for Security and Cooperation in Europe), xxiii, 82, 83, 84, 91, 96, 107, 116, 124

P

PRC (Permanent Representatives Committee), xxiii, 44
PSC (Political and Security Committee), xxiii, 44, 86, 115

R

Realpolitik, 19, 71, 72, 117
REC (Regional Economic Community), xxiii
REFORM (Regional Food Security and Risk Management Program), xxiii, 37
RUF (Revolutionary United Front), xxiii

S

SADC (Southern African Development Community), xxiii, 34, 37, 38, 62
SADD (Southern African Development Co-ordination Conference), xxiii
SASS (South African Secret Service), xxiii

SEC (Single European Act), xxiii, 85, 106, 121
SOC (Socialist Group), xxiii
sovereignty, 8, 19, 41, 70, 91, 93, 94, 95, 109, 114, 116, 122
SRO (Sub-Regional Office), xxiii

U

UEL (Group of the Unified European Left), xxiii
UN (United Nations), xxiii, 29, 36, 37, 40, 42, 44, 45, 50, 51, 52, 53, 54, 61, 63, 64, 65, 66, 74, 75, 86, 103, 107, 113, 117, 125, 126
UNAMSIL (United Nations Mission to Sierra Leone), xxiii, 125
UNDP (United Nations Development Program), xxiii, 53, 126
UNECA (United Nations Economic Commission for Africa), xxiii, 50, 51, 52, 117, 126
UNIOSIL (United Nations Integrated Office for Sierra Leone), xxiii
UNO (United Nations Organization), xxiii, 53
US (Untied States), xiii, xxiii, 63, 78, 79, 80, 81, 100, 102, 104, 105, 107, 126
USA (United States of America), xvii, xxiii, 26, 46, 59
USSR (Union of Sovereign Soviet Republics), xxiii, 76

W

WB (World Bank), xxiii, 75, 125
Weltpolitik, 19
WEU (Western European Union), xxiii, 76
WFP (World Food Program), xxiii

WTO (World Trade Organization), xxiii, 63, 76, 102
WWI (World War One), xxiii, 23, 24, 73, 112
WWII (World War Two), xxiii, 27, 40, 74, 75, 95, 100